Praise for
Make the Right Career Move

"Rachelle Canter's book, *Make the Right Career Move*, has insightful, incredibly helpful, essential career advancement information for senior executives, whether their focus is on getting a new job or a board position. I recommend this book highly to all executives looking to make the most of their careers."

> —Cheryl A. Fama
> Former President and CEO, Saint Francis Memorial Hospital, Catholic Healthcare West

"Rachelle Canter's book has insightful information for senior executives to consider. Although the book's focus is on employment, Canter's suggestions also could be relevant for board positions: for example, Canter's concept of creating a portfolio resume of career skills and accomplishments would be especially helpful for those senior executives seeking board level positions as part of their career advancement activities."

> —Lynn Shapiro Snyder
> Founder and President, Women Business Leaders of the U.S. Health Care Industry Foundation, National Health Care & Life Sciences Practice Leader, Epstein Becker & Green, P.C.
>
> Coauthor of *Answering the Call: Understanding the Duties, Risks, & Rewards of Corporate Governance.*

Make the Right Career Move

Make the Right Career Move

28 Critical Insights and Strategies to Land Your Dream Job

Rachelle J. Canter

John Wiley & Sons, Inc.

Published by John Wiley & Sons, Inc., Hoboken, New Jersey.
Published simultaneously in Canada.

For general information on our other products and services or for technical support, please contact our Customer Care Department within the United States at (800) 762-2974, outside the United States at (317) 572-3993 or fax (317) 572-4002.

Wiley also publishes its books in a variety of electronic formats. Some content that appears in print may not be available in electronic books. For more information about Wiley products, visit our web site at www.wiley.com.

Library of Congress Cataloging-in-Publication Data:

Canter, Rachelle J., 1948–

   Make the right career move : 28 critical insights and strategies to land
your dream job / Rachelle J. Canter.
      p.   cm.
   ISBN-13: 978-0-470-05236-5 (cloth)
   ISBN-10: 0-470-05236-8 (cloth)
   1. Job hunting.   2. Career development.   I. Title.
   HF5382.7.C363 2006
   650.14—dc22

                                                              2006013382

Printed in the United States of America.

10 9 8 7 6 5 4 3 2 1

To everyone who dreams of making the right career move:
You can do it!!

Acknowledgments

My deepest thanks to the entire team of friends, family, and colleagues who helped me, especially Erin McGrath for her invaluable strategic marketing advice and encouragement; David Catzel who suggested I write a book, and Diane Rosenblum who helped me get started; my mother, Matty Canter, and my cousin, Roberta Sabbath, for their incredible help and support throughout the process; Lauren Tanny; Rebecca Castleton; Mary Cranston; Marty Africa; Stewart Levine; Matt Feuer; Bernard Bushell; Mary Koelle; Linda Scales; Rebecca Crosby; Lou McClelland; Stephen Jones; Gregor Baer; David Bluhm; Nancy Siegel; Dan Richardson; Sue Hodges; Carol Hastings; Larry Richard; Lisa Mackey; Don Oppenheim; and all my wonderful clients who wrote testimonials and taught me so much about this work. And a special thanks to my dream editor, Laurie Frank Harting at Wiley and to my agent, James Levine, who brought us together.

Contents

STAGE THREE
FINDING THE RIGHT JOB

APPENDIXES

Introduction

Dan is a smart and personable, well-connected, and savvy executive with a great track record. He built his health care company through multimillion-dollar acquisitions, managed an aggressive two-year growth plan that achieved market leadership, and slashed operating costs by 15 percent. But Dan was bored by his industry and his job and, like many executives, didn't know how to make the career move he wanted.

Working with me, Dan expanded his view of what was possible in his career, developing the confidence to pursue his career dreams and the tools to realize them. He prepared a resume that presented his experience through succinct and quantified accomplishments. He defined a set of fact-based competitive advantages that demonstrated his unique qualifications and brand for each target job. He honed his interview skills, devising first-rate answers to questions and questions for interviewers. The result? Dan was quickly and successfully launched in an exciting new job and industry. He is now a different man, successful *and* satisfied! He sent an e-mail that read in part: "I would not have been a candidate for this job without your help. I don't mean that you were helpful to this process . . . you were essential. I cannot express strongly enough how grateful I am that I met you and that you took my case. You helped change my view of what was possible."

Dan might seem like one of the lucky ones because he reached success in his first career and transitioned to yet another successful and far more satisfying career. But it didn't happen overnight or without a lot of internal discovery and focused effort.

Whatever your situation—whether, like Dan, you have it made but want more from your career, or you have been displaced, outplaced, underemployed, never realized your full career potential, or just feel dissatisfied and trapped—this book can help you find work you love. These 28 crucial secrets of a successful job search will give you the tools and competitive edge to identify and land a personally fulfilling top job, as hundreds of people using these methods already have.

Make the Right Career Move is a book for all times, but especially for these times. An average of five or more career changes in the course of longer careers makes career change skills essential, yet no one teaches them. Busy schedules make the challenge still harder; the job and company demands on executives interfere with learning how to identify, find, and, most of all, land a dream job. Top jobs, especially personally satisfying ones, are scarce. Competition is fierce. Search consultants and employers seek round pegs for round holes. Wrong choices or job loss can spell career setbacks.

The stakes are high and the outcomes are uncertain. *Make the Right Career Move* provides the tools and skills to make the career moves you want. And though written for executives, attorneys, and other professionals, it provides crucial career information for all job seekers. *Make the Right Career Move* is a portable career coach that provides executives with a fast-track course in how to take control of their careers to achieve the real career success that comes from true career satisfaction. A job and career you love await you.

DEFINING THE RIGHT JOB

Chapter 1

Imagine Career Possibilities

Secret: The major obstacle to your
dream job is in your head.

The primary obstacle to a successful job search lies within, in limited and limiting self-perceptions about your career. A positive mind-set about your career possibilities is essential to finding a top job. Most executives perceive job search obstacles as external: a poor economy, the resistance of employers and search consultants to putting an executive into a different job or industry, an underdeveloped network. This is wrong. The biggest obstacle to a successful career move is internal—a failure of imagination. Change your beliefs to change your future.

How do you go from the top to more? First, dispense with the idea that the process begins with "doing," at least in the traditional sense of taking action. Finding inspiration and passion is a psychological and spiritual journey. It requires getting rid of the primary obstacles that block us from achieving our dreams. Those obstacles are in the most unexpected place: the stories we tell.

Collective Explanations

Sometimes, limiting stories are widely shared. Have you ever noticed that when people say "The truth is . . ." what follows is always some kind of limitation or obstacle? "The truth is" restricts what is or could be. "The truth is . . . there are just no opportunities for advertising executives these days." "The truth is . . . the only way to

3

get ahead in high tech is to be utterly ruthless and use others to advance your own career." "The truth is . . . good guys finish last."

Evidence for this limiting point of view abounds. Dramatic stories about people losing jobs and finding nothing to replace them sell newspapers. Horror stories about bad bosses and bad markets fill magazines and talk shows. An embittered friend, neighbor, or relative eagerly shares the scars of a particularly bad work experience. A burned-out colleague opts for early retirement and quits the game altogether. Self-help books use scare tactics to sell the one right way to avoid career disaster.

The point is that these "truth"-ful explanations are collective versions of stories about limitations and obstacles. They have the effect of discouraging effort and preventing achievement and success.

Individual Success and Failure Stories

The stories that limit us are both individual and collective: Stories about the way the world is are one form of limiting belief; stories about our own successes and failures are another.

The stories we tell can empower or disempower us. People who attribute their successes to their own efforts or abilities—things they can control—strive harder and longer, feel greater pride in their achievements, and find greater success. Those who attribute their failures (or successes) to outside influences such as luck or the situation have a diminished sense of power and less motivation to strive or persist because things that dictate successful and unsuccessful outcomes are beyond their control.

The empowering and disempowering stories we tell are an appropriate place to begin the journey to find a dream job. We drag around our pasts in the form of justifications, excuses, and baggage that explains how we got where we are and why we cannot go further, be more, or enjoy more than we do. When our future is limited by our past and its stories, it can be no bigger or richer than the limited possibilities of that past.

Listen to a story about a client of mine whose experiences illustrate this.

The Pre-CEO Story: The Story of George

I knew within 10 minutes of meeting George that he had all the makings of the CEO he aspired to be. He was smart, articulate, optimistic, polished, driven but calm. He had excellent interpersonal skills and well-honed financial and operating expertise. He had a great sense of humor. His complaint? He was 44 and had not been CEO.

As George saw it, he had made choices in favor of his family, not his career. He had chosen to raise his children in a small town. He had selected a position that required minimal commute time. And most important, he had chosen to spend time with his wife and young children. He was glad for the time he had spent with his family but worried that his greatest career ambitions had been thwarted.

Halfway through our meeting, George began to reiterate the reasons he hadn't been a CEO yet, when I interrupted him, saying, "Drop the story, George. You had good reasons for the decisions you made. You won't have that time again with your wife and kids. Now you're ready to make new decisions. Drop the story. It isn't serving you."

My words startled him, but he instantly knew that repeating this story was actually sapping his energy and focus and keeping him from realizing his dreams.

Dropping the story and focusing on how to identify and find his dream job put him very quickly into a new industry he longed to join and on a fast track to the CEO he has now become.

Prior success may create its own limiting story. George's success led him to conclude that the best of his career was behind him, that he had had his one big shot at success and missed it. His story about how his focus on his family had cost him the chance to realize his career dreams threatened to keep his dreams permanently out of reach. These stories supported inaction and were in danger of becoming self-fulfilling prophecies.

Identify Your Stories

Many highly successful executive clients seek help, feeling dispirited, burned out, fed up, trapped. Their sights are limited and their energy and enthusiasm sapped. Many doubt their considerable abilities.

The prospect of fulfilling and enjoyable work seems remote. Inspiring work seems unattainable. They'd settle for work that isn't, as they've variously described it, "soulless," "mind-numbing," or "gut-wrenching." That's not good enough, and that's not what this book is about.

You cannot go straight from despair or dissatisfaction to inspiration. Finding your dream job is a process, similar to clearing a site before laying the foundation. You must clear the mental underbrush of limiting stories about your career before you can envision your own possibilities.

What stories do you tell yourself and others about your own successes and failures? How do these interpretations of the past limit your aspirations, inspirations, and efforts? Do you have a story about not being good enough to succeed, so that eventually and inevitably you screw things up after an initial success? Do you have a story about your being a plodder whose success is entirely due to working harder than anyone else? Is your story about how you peaked at 16, in a haze of student leadership and popularity contests? What are you getting out of these stories? What are the stories costing you?

Behavior is controlled by its consequences. You wouldn't continue to tell your stories if they weren't eliciting some positive results, even if you are not consciously aware of those results. What positive outcomes are provided by telling the stories? Sympathy or admiration for your struggles? A way to avoid the risks or efforts necessary to pursue your dreams? A sense of self-worth and conviction of your loyalty to others? There are many positive rewards as well as costs attached to your stories; becoming aware of them is an important step toward letting go of your stories.

For example, the story about being a hardworking plodder may mean that others appreciate you for your superhuman efforts: "Isn't Cynthia incredible? She works harder and cares more about her work product than anyone else." The respect and appreciation may make you feel superior, but at the cost of exhaustion and burnout.

The first step is to recognize the stories you tell about yourself. This is a challenge because stories often hide in plain sight. They define your perception of reality; they are the lens through which you see the world. That's why it's critical to expose them for what they are: interpretations of reality rather than reality.

You cannot rid yourself of beliefs or stories that are holding you back if you aren't conscious of what they are. The next sections provide you with three simple worksheets to identify and eliminate your stories.

Develop Your List of Stories

The first step in this process is to identify your stories. How do you explain your successes and failures? Luck? Effort? Ability? Circumstance? A positive attitude? Is your fast-track career based on outperforming the competition? A series of lucky breaks? Are you a perfectionist who cannot tolerate the compromises others make to produce shoddy work? Did you pay the price with a competitive boss who was threatened by you and maneuvered your ouster? Look for themes that emerge from your explanations of moves throughout your career.

See how George completed the List of Stories Worksheet. In the pre-CEO story, George's explanation was "I missed my big chance in my career and I will never get it back." To record your own stories, turn to the back of the book. Blank copies of all worksheets

---

List of Stories Worksheet

- **Story #1:** You get one shot at the C-suite: I missed my big career chance and I'll never get it back.
- **Story #2:** You can't have a big career and a happy family.
- **Story #3:** Forty-four is too old to become CEO.
- **Story #4:**
- **Story #5:**
- **Story #6:**
- **Story #7:**
- **Story #8:**
- **Story #9:**

---

and exercises throughout the book are in Appendix F so you can copy and use them.

Let Go of Your Stories

It's one thing to identify the stories that have colored your views of yourself and what is possible in your life and career. But how do you let go of them? Is it really so simple to identify the costs and benefits and an action step to drop the story? People spend years in therapy working on these issues.

This book is not about psychotherapy. It's about choice and commitment. You have a choice about how you view things. You can choose to ignore the stories, or you can choose to continue to support them.

It all boils down to making a choice and affirming that choice again and again. You cannot change the past, but you can learn from it. Most important, you can make a different choice today. That's really all any of us has: the choices we make today. You know where your stories have gotten you. Are you ready to try a different path?

Complete the Cost/Benefit Analysis Worksheet in Appendix F to evaluate the stories you identified in the List of Stories Worksheet, as well as what you will do to let go of this story. Don't rush to complete this exercise because the stories are often so entrenched that we aren't aware of their profound impact on us and our work choices and possibilities. Taking time to understand the stories and their positive and negative consequences will help you move on. The Cost/Benefit Analysis Worksheet at the bottom of the page depicts George's answers.

Recognizing that your interpretations of the past are stories that often limit you can provide access to a whole new world of possibilities you can imagine and pursue.

Breaking Free of the Past: The Story of Todd

In a seminar he was attending, Todd engaged in a lengthy and heated exchange with the leader. Todd explained that his entire life had been scarred by a demanding father. His father imposed such unrealistic expectations that Todd, who was smart and Ivy

Cost/Benefit Analysis Worksheet

Story	Costs	Benefits	Steps to Give It Up
One shot at C-suite: missed my big chance	Despair, scarcity mentality	Avoid hard work of job search	Remind self it's just a story; start work on resume and career plan; focus on *this* shot at C-suite
Big career and happy family incompatible	Regret at choice, resentment toward family	Self-sacrificing good guy: gave up my dreams for family	Focus on present, not past, and on choices to maximize career satisfaction today
44 is too old to be CEO	Feelings of discouragement and powerlessness	Avoid risk of competition for what I want	Look at stats on CEO ages, talk to recruiters

League-educated, had never been able to get or keep a good job, much less an inspiring one, because his father always made him feel like a failure.

As a specific example of his father's reign of terror, Todd described how his father had taught him to read at an early age, making him repeat sentences again and again until he got them right. The leader listened carefully to this story and pointed out the difference between what really happened—the objective facts—and the interpretations or stories Todd had made up about what happened. The leader said, "Another way to look at that story is 'My father loved me so much he spent time making sure I learned to read correctly.' How would it feel to have lived a life inside that story instead of the one you chose?"

Todd's story about his father led him to conclude, "I'm not good enough." What possible benefit or reward was he getting from a story that made him so unhappy? First, he didn't have to put himself out there to compete for opportunities he believed he could never win. Second, people felt sorry for him and paid attention to his "poor me" stories. The costs? Satisfying work and lucrative compensation are obvious costs, as well as a sense of vitality.

Your next step is to determine the costs and benefits of your own stories. Then determine if you want to let go of them. If you do, decide on the steps you will take. Often the appropriate first step is to consciously refrain from repeating the same tired stories to yourself or others. Both empowering and disempowering stories can have a big impact on your future rather than simply recounting your past.

Envisioning Your Possibilities

Once you strip away the limiting beliefs, anything is possible. Todd's letting go of the story of the critical father led him to satisfying work in political publishing; George's letting go of the story of why he hadn't been a CEO initiated a process that led to the CEO's office.

You have many more possibilities for your career than you now realize. The goal of this book is to help you recognize your possibilities and realize them. The first step is to find a possibility for your career that inspires you to action. This inspiration—a rediscovered source of joy and excitement in your work—is what will motivate the steps you take to reach your goal. A possibility creates something exciting to move toward rather than something to escape from. A possibility transforms the necessary steps to reach your goal from work into progress. There's a world of difference between the two.

Possibilities Exercise

How do you start thinking about possibilities? One way is to think of times when you were inspired by your work or other activities. Think of three times you were engaged in work that lit you up, turned you on. Describe why the work was important to you, what talents and expertise it called on, and what objectives—personal and professional—you met. What are the common themes in these three experiences? Are they the goals of the work, the kind of people you worked with, your role, the setting (an airport, forest, boardroom, or manufacturing plant), or some other factor?

Use the blank Possibilities Worksheet in Appendix F to get you started. Record each activity you enjoyed, along with what it was you particularly enjoyed about it. Continue the exploration by identifying and recording additional stories about activities and projects you enjoyed throughout your life. Specifically, consider:

- Three work projects you engaged in as an adult
- Two favorite volunteer or extracurricular projects or activities you did as an adult or adolescent
- Two examples of things you loved to do and did well as an adolescent
- Two examples of things you loved to do and did well up to age 13

Use the themes you uncover in doing this exercise to point you toward your own possibility. Once you have completed the worksheet,

Possibilities Worksheet

Event or Activity	Why Did You Enjoy It?
Work #1: Opening new hospital	Opportunity to build something from scratch
Work #2: Develop new inpatient service	Creating something new, serving customers better
Work #3:	
Extracurricular #1: Leading task force to evaluate and redefine board role for theater company	Reinventing board role and improving board's effectiveness: like to improve things
Extracurricular #2:	
Adolescent #1: Senior class officer	Leadership role, making things happen
Adolescent #2:	
Childhood #1:	
Childhood #2:	

look for common themes in the examples. Do you now have a clearer vision of your inspiring possibility?

Reimagining a Career: The Story of Mary

Mary is a health care executive. She was frustrated by the current health care environment and its focus on cost containment rather than development and customer service. She saw little of interest in the health care arena and was eager to move out of the industry in which she had spent more than 20 years.

To focus her new career search, Mary identified past work experiences she had enjoyed: two start-up business projects; leading a local theater board task force to reexamine and reinvent the role of the board in fund-raising, administration, and repertory choices for the theater company; and serving as an officer of her high school class.

The Possibilities Worksheet depicts Mary's responses. The three exciting pieces of work had given her a long-forgotten experience of enthusiasm and delight. She realized that building something was critical to an inspiring career possibility for her future. And her high school example reminded her of her long-standing enjoyment of leadership roles and the ability to make things happen.

Before exploring how to turn possibilities into specific targets instead of fanciful ideas, we will examine important factors that affect the search for your dream job: the psychological obstacles that may be getting in the way of finding your dream job, the all-important element of personal career satisfaction, and the very definition of what that dream job is.

Chapter 2

Three Executive Obstacles to Job Search

Secret: The very executive habits that create work success can spell job search failure.

Craig is a superstar CEO: a corporate wunderkind with an Ivy League pedigree who achieved major success in two very different industries by age 30. He is a Wall Street legend, the subject of a Harvard Business School case, a corporate executive, an investment banker, and an entrepreneur. The common theme in his career has been reinventing businesses—and success after success.

By his mid-50s, he'd sold a major business and was looking for his next career, afraid the best was behind him. Having exceeded most people's dreams of success, recognition, wealth, and power, he nevertheless worried about the future. He wanted to be in the middle of the fray, leading a major arts center or governmental agency, not in the peripheral role of board member.

Many executives would be thrilled to have achieved what Craig had and be content to rest on their laurels. But Craig, ever the achiever, was restless and dissatisfied. Instead of searching for the perfect job for himself, he was waiting for someone to find him for the perfect job. Though he was too proud to admit to frustration, he was clearly unhappy because he had so much to contribute and no one was extending offers to him.

This uncharacteristically passive approach to his career was based on a mistaken assumption about how career moves happen.

Craig figured that his impressive reputation and contacts would lead others to him. He was waiting to be found and asked. But reputation and contacts do not guarantee a great new role, especially if the sought-after new role represents a marked shift in direction.

Craig needed to put himself back in the game, as he had always done in the past, instead of waiting to be asked to join. He didn't want to be relegated to the sidelines, but he didn't know what to do or where to go. And he was laboring under another common misconception: that a person gets one big chance at success and he had already had his.

Complicating matters, some of the things that made him an effective CEO made it more difficult to find new career inspiration. He was used to reasoning his way quickly out of situations and taking quick and decisive action. He was used to being smarter than anyone else, which made it hard to listen to advice. He was also used to being the expert and intimidating others into silence. He was unwilling or unable to ask for help.

Three Obstacles to Inspiring Possibilities

Craig's story illustrates three common obstacles faced by executives: *knowing it all*, *instant answers*, and *invulnerability*. Executives are used to having the answers, figuring things out themselves, and taking action—all impediments to finding inspiring work.

Let's dispense quickly with all three:

1. *The obstacle of knowing it all:* You don't know it all even if you're smarter and more successful than other people. If you did, you wouldn't be dissatisfied with where you are. If it were so easy to find inspiring work, everyone would love his or her job, and people like me wouldn't be in business. There's no shame in not knowing everything. Giving yourself permission to not know it all frees you to ask questions and find answers that can guide you toward inspiring work.

2. *The obstacle of instant answers:* Finding a career possibility that inspires takes reflection and takes time. Applying the can-do

and fast approach you use with other problems won't work here. Too many executives operate under the misguided notion that inspiring work is the result of revelation, a blinding and instant knowledge of your life's purpose.

This notion fits nicely with executives' self-concept as people who make things happen fast. Finding an inspiring life purpose is almost always the result of the gradual accumulation of information through self-exploration. If you're waiting for a revelation, you're likely to be waiting a long, long time—maybe forever. This book breaks the necessary reflection and exploration into bite-size pieces, so you can develop insights and momentum in the process while maintaining a demanding schedule and job.

3. *The obstacle of invulnerability:* No one is invulnerable, but executives often forget this is so. Equating invulnerability with strength and leadership, and vulnerability with weakness, perpetuates the appearance of strength. While it may protect you from those you believe would take advantage of you, it also locks you in a box the size of your current insights and knowledge.

The illusion of invulnerability can keep you from work you love, by depriving you of honest feedback and useful two-way communication. If you can't look to others for assistance, you're apt to stay stuck.

The inability to ask for help is one of the most career-threatening mistakes executives make. Take this opportunity to experience the paradox of the strength that comes from acknowledging limitation. Finding and realizing your greatest career possibility is more than a one-person job. What's it going to be: your pride or your happiness?

Craig's discomfort with listening instead of leading conversations and his resistance to feedback were an open secret. His colleagues and subordinates, even his friends did not dare say it to him. The need to seem self-sufficient and indomitable kept others at a distance and a new career out of reach. What's so unfortunate is that when his dream job materialized, he was unprepared to take the necessary steps, such as letting the search committee or influential contacts know of his interest and availability. As experienced and accomplished as he was and is, his dream job slipped through his fingers.

Characteristic executive habits of thought and style can interfere with your job search. Recognizing the need to learn how to make career moves is essential to a successful job search. Similarly, the habit of expecting instant answers at work doesn't lend itself to the thoughtful exploration required of career or job change. And the belief in personal invulnerability flies in the face of securing the necessary help to create change outside your area of expertise. Start the process by letting go of these counterproductive habits.

Chapter 3

Career Satisfaction: The Elusive and Essential Ingredient of the Right Move

---

Secret: The right move is not necessarily "up."

Career Satisfaction: Why It Matters

Career satisfaction is a critical but often overlooked ingredient of happiness and well-being. Defining the ideal job, exploring career options, and making the right decisions for your life begin here. If you are not happy with your work, you cannot have a truly successful career, no matter how hard you work or how much money you make.

For many executives whose career decisions have not been guided or influenced by considerations of career satisfaction and who find themselves dissatisfied with their success, the right move may be in any direction, not just up the ladder they no longer enjoy. The right job may entail a different kind of move; personal career satisfaction is essential to making that right move.

A great career is no accident. It's more than wishing, hoping, or serendipity. Whether seeking your 1st, 2nd, or 20th chance at an extraordinary career, it begins with priorities. Priorities provide a clear vision of what you want and where you are headed.

Many people have detailed lists of what they are looking for in a mate. Yet when asked to provide a similarly detailed list of the characteristics of their ideal job, they rely on clichés. This is a mistake. Numerous studies show that a good fit between the person and the job leads to career satisfaction, stability, and success. Defining the causes and sources of career satisfaction will put you on the right path to attaining it.

For example, a list of ideal job essentials might include a company whose mission is to improve the health of customers; an opportunity to build a new division; an aggressive and clear strategic plan for the company; an explicit succession plan for becoming president; a commute of under one hour; no more than 25 percent travel; an action-oriented, nonbureaucratic environment; a team environment; and a management team filled with people with advanced degrees.

A litigator at a major San Francisco law firm is the rare person (and certainly the rare lawyer and litigator) who loves her work. She's not an aggressive sort who thrives on combat. She wears her adversarial role lightly but surely. When I asked why she enjoys her work, she replied, "I don't do it for the money."

Although she is well compensated and enjoys the financial rewards, it's not what motivates her. "On the bad days, there's not enough money to make up for it, and on the good days, the money is irrelevant." She has found work that satisfies her own needs and goals. Her satisfaction is a major factor in her success and happiness.

Chapter 4

Turn Career Possibilities
into Targets

Secret: The ideal job lies at the intersection
of skills, goals, and satisfiers.

How do you go from an inspiring, if somewhat vague, possibility to a specific target? Revelations are rare, but information is plentiful. You already know a great deal about your ideal job. You just lack a way to simplify and organize the information into a usable framework. Showing you how to do this is the goal of this chapter.

For the 99 percent of you who never experience a revelation about your life's work, this step-by-step process from possibilities to targets is the best route to the same goal. If, like many of my clients, you fear doing it wrong, I'll let you in on a secret: There is no perfect way of doing it "right." There's just doing it.

Look for your ideal job at the intersection of your skills, goals, satisfiers, and dissatisfiers. Step-by-step investigation of these elements of the right fit provides a simple and effective way to define your future. Follow the simple steps in A Step-by-Step Guide to Defining Your Ideal Job to define your ideal job and turn your possibility into something you can pursue and land.

The Consequences of Not Defining Priorities:
The Story of Tim's Dad

Tim was a young insurance executive in his early 30s who had created a new insurance product that was generating big sales for his

A Step-by-Step Guide to Defining Your Ideal Job

- Assess Skills: What are your greatest and most personally enjoyable skills?
- Assess Goals: What are your primary career, relationship, and personal development goals?
- Assess Satisfiers and Dissatisfiers: What specific aspects of each job, work setting, role, result, colleagues, and corporate culture do you like and dislike most?
- Record up to 5 greatest and most enjoyable skills, up to 4 priority goals, and up to 10 most critical satisfiers or dissatisfiers on the Ideal Job Factors Worksheet.
- Consider your portfolio career, that is, the impact of accomplishments that are highly marketable and that may suggest a particular and possibly alternative direction for the use of your talents and turning your possibility into a job target.
- Narrow the Ideal Job Factors to the 10 most personally important or critical factors using a forced ranking technique. List them on the Ranked Ideal Job Factors Worksheet.
- Identify and evaluate three or more possible straw men, jobs that fit your top ideal job criteria and your portfolio career on the Straw Men Worksheet.
- Select your top job scenario. That's your Ideal Job target.

company. He was being groomed for a top spot: plum assignments on high-visibility task forces that provided exposure to the senior officers of the company, invitations to participate in individualized leadership training with the company's consultant for executive development, on the list of the company's top 50 high-potential executives.

Despite the success and recognition, Tim was burned out and looking for a new challenge. He was motivated to do so by fear: He had watched his father spend more than 35 years at one company and quit six months prior to retirement with full benefits. His father returned from summer vacation and tendered his resignation. Six months short of freedom after working more than 35 years! It was crazy, and Tim told him so. "Why?" he asked. And his father replied, "Because I realized I couldn't take one more day."

Tim wasn't about to repeat his father's mistake. He'd been stuck in a lucrative but dull job, bored but secure. His father's quitting jolted him out of the lull he'd been in careerwise. He had some vague dreams about doing work that excited him. But vague dreams didn't translate into a concrete job target, much less a plan of action. He saw insurance as a useful product, but Tim wanted to sell something he loved, like motorcycles, or believed in, like medical equipment for cancer patients.

The Ideal Job

Let's demystify the process of defining your ideal job. The ideal job lies at the intersection of skills, interests, strengths and weaknesses, accomplishments, values, style, life and career goals, and job satisfiers and dissatisfiers. The Ideal Job diagram provides a picture of this.

This chapter provides a simplified and streamlined approach to defining your ideal job. It includes a case example (Appendix A) using this approach, reviewing the eight-step targeting process previously discussed. Use this example to guide you through the process.

The focus of the targeting process is on skills, goals, and satisfiers and dissatisfiers. The primary questions to answer are:

- *Skills:* What are your greatest and most personally enjoyable skills?
- *Goals:* What are your primary career, relationship, and personal development goals?
- *Satisfiers and Dissatisfiers:* What specific aspects of each job, work setting, role, result, colleagues, and corporate culture do you like and dislike most?

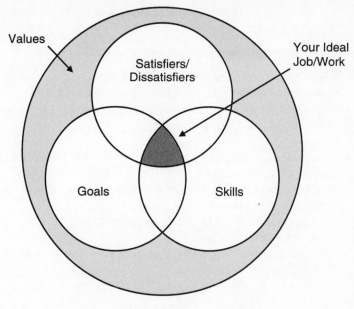

The Ideal Job

Skills

An inspiring career possibility involves things you do well and love to do. Read the first page of the Skills Inventory Worksheet for an overview of the skills exercise. Worksheets are included at the back of the book so you can copy and use them.

The Skills Inventory Worksheet lists your greatest skills, bodies of knowledge, and personal strengths. What are you particularly good at? Promoting the firm's products and services? Writing briefs? Managing client portfolios? Strategic planning? Budgeting? Negotiating settlements? The skills are arranged by functional area, with room to add specific skills, especially higher level skills, within a functional area. At what specific skills do you excel? (Appendix A illustrates this step.)

What substantive knowledge have you gained through your work? Bodies of knowledge might include foreign or computer languages, experience with a particular forecasting model, expertise in employment litigation or real estate law, knowledge of specific federal regulations or stock option plans. Finally, what personal

Skills Inventory Worksheet

The first step in the job search process is to determine where you are now. There are three kinds of attributes you will assess:

- Skills: What you can do (e.g., write, analyze, program, sell)
- Knowledge: What you know about or know how to do
- Personal Strengths: Characteristics unique to you (e.g., creative, cooperative, motivated, energetic)

A. Review the lists of SKILLS, KNOWLEDGE, and PERSONAL STRENGTHS on the following pages.
B. Place a check mark in the column that best describes your level of proficiency using the following scale:
   1 = Basic: general working knowledge of concepts, policies, procedures, or practices
   2 = Intermediate: full working knowledge of concepts, policies, procedures, or practices
   3 = Advanced: detailed knowledge of concepts, policies, procedures, or practices
C. Include additional attributes you have that are not listed.
D. Leave blank attributes with which you are unfamiliar or that you feel you don't have.
E. Record all ratings of 3 (Advanced) on the Summary page.
F. Circle all items on the Summary page that you enjoy using. These are your priority skills, areas of knowledge, and personal strengths.

SKILLS
   1 = Basic
   2 = Intermediate
   3 = Advanced

Supervison/Management

1 2 3
___ ___ ___ Allocating resources
___ ___ ___ Analyzing/assessing
___ ___ ___ Balancing business and staff needs
___ ___ ___ Budgeting
___ ___ ___ Communicating relevant information
___ ___ ___ Counseling/coaching
___ ___ ___ Delegating
___ ___ ___ Developing staff

1 2 3
___ ___ ___ Directing others
___ ___ ___ Hiring staff
___ ___ ___ Implementing changes
___ ___ ___ Implementing policies
___ ___ ___ Initiating action
___ ___ ___ Integrating company objectives
___ ___ ___ Interviewing
___ ___ ___ Leading meetings
___ ___ ___ Making decisions

1 2 3

_ _ _ Managing staff performance
_ _ _ Monitoring productivity
_ _ _ Motivating
_ _ _ Negotiating
_ _ _ Organizing/coordinating
_ _ _ Planning
_ _ _ Public speaking
_ _ _ Scheduling
_ _ _ Selecting staff/planning staffing needs

1 2 3

_ _ _ Solving problems
_ _ _ Strategizing
_ _ _ Time management
_ _ _ Writing performance plans/reviews
_ _ _ Writing proposals
_ _ _ _____
_ _ _ _____
_ _ _ _____

Communication

1 2 3

_ _ _ Composing correspondence/written material
_ _ _ Defining
_ _ _ Describing
_ _ _ Drawing/illustrating
_ _ _ Editing
_ _ _ Explaining
_ _ _ Expressing yourself clearly
_ _ _ Interpreting
_ _ _ Listening effectively
_ _ _ Proofreading

1 2 3

_ _ _ Public speaking
_ _ _ Publicizing
_ _ _ Reporting
_ _ _ Responding to inquiries
_ _ _ Spelling
_ _ _ Teaching/training others
_ _ _ Using correct grammar
_ _ _ Writing clearly
_ _ _ _____
_ _ _ _____
_ _ _ _____

Customer Relations

1 2 3

_ _ _ Being courteous
_ _ _ Being tactful/diplomatic
_ _ _ Building rapport
_ _ _ Calming irate customers
_ _ _ Determining customer needs
_ _ _ Expressing yourself clearly
_ _ _ Following through on communications
_ _ _ Listening effectively
_ _ _ Promoting firm's image

1 2 3

_ _ _ Promoting firm's products and services
_ _ _ Remembering and using customers' names
_ _ _ Resolving problems
_ _ _ Responding to inquiries
_ _ _ Using effective telephone techniques
_ _ _ _____
_ _ _ _____
_ _ _ _____

(continued)

Skills Inventory Worksheet (*Continued*)

Financial/Mathematical

1 2 3
___ ___ ___ Analyzing/assessing
___ ___ ___ Auditing
___ ___ ___ Calculating
___ ___ ___ Comparing
___ ___ ___ Computing
___ ___ ___ Evaluating

1 2 3
___ ___ ___ Problem solving
___ ___ ___ Projecting
___ ___ ___ _____
___ ___ ___ _____
___ ___ ___ _____

Research/Analytical

1 2 3
___ ___ ___ Analyzing/assessing
        data/statistics
___ ___ ___ Classifying
___ ___ ___ Compiling data
___ ___ ___ Documenting
___ ___ ___ Evaluating
___ ___ ___ Hypothesizing
___ ___ ___ Investigating

1 2 3
___ ___ ___ Monitoring
___ ___ ___ Organizing/coordinating
___ ___ ___ Problem solving
___ ___ ___ Researching
___ ___ ___ Systematizing
___ ___ ___ _____
___ ___ ___ _____
___ ___ ___ _____

Sales/Marketing

1 2 3
___ ___ ___ Analyzing/assessing
        customers' needs
___ ___ ___ Asking probing questions
___ ___ ___ Closing a sale
___ ___ ___ Describing product
        features
___ ___ ___ Developing new product
        ideas
___ ___ ___ Evaluating
___ ___ ___ Managing client portfolios
___ ___ ___ Market planning

1 2 3
___ ___ ___ Market research
___ ___ ___ Marketing/direct response
___ ___ ___ Meeting quotas
___ ___ ___ Negotiating
___ ___ ___ Organizing/coordinating
___ ___ ___ Overcoming objections
___ ___ ___ Selling benefits of products
___ ___ ___ Setting goals/objectives
___ ___ ___ _____
___ ___ ___ _____
___ ___ ___ _____

Skills Inventory Worksheet (*Continued*)

Data Processing/Systems

1 2 3

____ Analyzing application
systems

____ Analyzing operating
systems and hardware

____ Capacity planning

____ Creating systems
specifications

____ Designing databases

____ Modifying package
software

____ Monitoring vendors

____ Programming languages
and methods

____ Project planning and
control

____ Providing product
support/user liaison

1 2 3

____ Quality control

____ Security planning

____ Structured analysis

____ Structured design

____ Structured tests

____ Systems programming

____ Technical writing: systems
documentation

____ Technical writing: user
training/tutorials

____ _____

____ _____

____ _____

____ _____

Personal Computers

Use the blank spaces to list specific packages you are familiar with.

1 2 3 Database packages

____ _____

____ _____

____ _____

1 2 3 Integrated packages (e.g.,
Lotus 123)

____ _____

____ _____

____ _____

1 2 3 Electronic spreadsheets

____ _____

____ _____

____ _____

1 2 3 Word processing packages

____ _____

____ _____

____ _____

(continued)

KNOWLEDGE

Because each person has acquired a *unique* body of knowledge, you must choose, enumerate, and evaluate what you know.

Examples of knowledge you might list are:

Foreign language fluency
Real estate law
Benefits planning
Computer languages

1 = Basic
2 = Intermediate
3 = Advanced

1 2 3

— — — _____

— — — _____

— — — _____

— — — _____

— — — _____

— — — _____

— — — _____

— — — _____

— — — _____

Skills Inventory Worksheet *(Continued)*

PERSONAL STRENGTHS

1 = Basic
2 = Intermediate
3 = Advanced

1 2 3

__ __ __ Accepting supervision
__ __ __ Achieving goals/results
__ __ __ Being cooperative
__ __ __ Being dependable
__ __ __ Being diplomatic
__ __ __ Being discreet
__ __ __ Being flexible
__ __ __ Being impartial
__ __ __ Being objective
__ __ __ Being patient
__ __ __ Being resourceful
__ __ __ Being tactful
__ __ __ Being tolerant
__ __ __ Building rapport
__ __ __ Compromising
__ __ __ Contributing ideas
__ __ __ Evaluating alternatives

1 2 3

__ __ __ Following through on
commitments
__ __ __ Gaining cooperation of
others
__ __ __ Inspiring confidence
__ __ __ Making decisions
__ __ __ Managing time
__ __ __ Motivating others
__ __ __ Persuading and influencing
others
__ __ __ Remaining calm under
pressure
__ __ __ Setting priorities
__ __ __ _____
__ __ __ _____
__ __ __ _____

(continued)

Skills Inventory Worksheet *(Continued)*

SUMMARY

Now that you have taken inventory of your skills, summarize the information. Record your greatest skills, bodies of knowledge, and personal strengths (Level 3) on this sheet. Circle those that you most enjoy using.

Skills: _____   _____

                _____   _____

                _____   _____

                _____   _____

                _____   _____

Knowledge: _____   _____

                _____   _____

                _____   _____

                _____   _____

Personal Strengths: _____   _____

                _____   _____

                _____   _____

                _____   _____

                _____   _____

strengths or characteristics distinguish you? Do you excel at being diplomatic? Motivating others? Being impartial? Organizing information? Contributing creative ideas?

Look for the rating of 3, which denotes advanced levels of skill, knowledge, and strength. Because this tool is used by people in all fields, don't worry if entire pages don't rate one skill as a 3.

Identifying skills is only the first step. In all likelihood, you excel at some things you detest. Because the ideal job, by definition, includes things you enjoy doing, the next step is to identify the subset of those skills, strengths, and areas of knowledge that you most enjoy using. Circle these greatest and most enjoyable skills on the Summary page of the Skills Inventory Worksheet.

Goals

The ideal job not only meets your long-term career goals, but works in the context of your larger life goals. Career goals are the major focus: What is it you want to achieve in your career? Relationship goals provide an opportunity to define your objectives for personal relationships with family, friends, and others. Personal development goals refer to extracurricular goals such as learning to play the guitar, sail around the world, or work out regularly. Select the top priority goals among all goals identified in these three areas. Use the Goal Planning Worksheet in the appendix to identify and prioritize your career, relationship, and personal development goals. (See Appendix A for a detailed example of goal identification.)

Identify conflicts or dependencies among the priority goals: Is reaching one goal at odds with reaching another, or is reaching one apt to increase the chances to reach another? For example, a career goal of being CEO of a Fortune 500 company is likely to conflict with a relationship goal of spending nights and weekends with the family, but may be likely to increase the chances of learning to play golf well.

This exercise affords an opportunity to consider just what place your career occupies in the context of your life and all your career,

Goal Planning Worksheet

List your primary goals in each of three areas: career, relationships, and personal development.

What is your conception of the ideal attainments in your **CAREER?** Be as free and specific as possible in selecting these goals. Summarize them below.

> Examples: I want to become president of my own company.
>
> I want to sit on the board of a Fortune 500 company.
>
> I want to be recognized as an expert in the financial services industry.
>
> I want to lead project teams managing major system conversions.

1.

2.

3.

4.

What is your conception of ideal attainments in your **PERSONAL RELATIONSHIPS?** Be as free as possible in selecting these goals. Summarize below.

> Examples: I want to spend nights and weekends with my family.
>
> I want children.
>
> I want to coach my daughter's soccer team.

1.

2.

3.

4.

Goal Planning Worksheet (*Continued*)

What is your conception of ideal attainments in your **PERSONAL DEVELOPMENT AND LEARNING?** Be as free as possible in selecting these goals. Summarize below.

Examples: I want to learn to fly an airplane.

I want to practice yoga.

I want to exercise three times a week.

I want to learn Spanish.

1.

2.

3.

4.

GOAL PRIORITIES: Select the goals from the previous three items that seem most important to you at this time. Do not choose more than four. Rank order them in terms of importance, with 1 being the most important.

1.

2.

3.

4.

POTENTIAL GOAL CONFLICTS AND DEPENDENCIES: One of the major deterrents to goal accomplishment is conflict between goals. The person who ignores the potential conflicts between job and family, for example, will probably end up abandoning goals because of the either/or nature of many decisions. In some cases, working on one goal can help you reach another goal (goal dependencies). For example, learning to windsurf (a personal development goal) may facilitate increasing your network of friends (a relationship goal). List the goal conflicts and positive goal dependencies below.

(continued)

GOAL CONFLICTS

1.

2.

3.

GOAL DEPENDENCIES

1.

2.

3.

IMPLICATIONS FOR ACTION: What are the implications for career planning and management of your goal priorities, conflicts, and dependencies (e.g., a job that requires limited travel so you can spend nights and weekends with family)?

1.

2.

3.

relationship, and personal goals. What are your priorities at this point in your career, and what are the implications for career choice?

Satisfiers and Dissatisfiers as the Key to Fit: The Story of Bill

This case study illustrates the importance of using satisfiers and dissatisfiers to define the characteristics of a personally ideal job.

Bill is a senior corporate communications executive who has helped CEOs in major corporations out of almost every imaginable crisis, from a chemical spill at a major refinery to an infectious disease outbreak at a major medical center to rescuing an international law firm from the brink of extinction.

Raised in a military family that moved around the world, comfortable with change, and happiest in the eye of the storm, Bill was born to think and talk people out of disasters. As he explored his career successes and frustrations, he saw that the ability to move quickly and decisively was central to his success and satisfaction.

Working for a strong CEO with a lot of centralized authority, as a client or an employee, was a perfect fit for Bill's action-oriented style. His prior employer, a big law firm, was not a great fit. He hated the protracted, consensus-based decision-making process in a partnership. The oversized egos frustrated him. And partners' belief in their superiority in matters of communication as well as law hampered his attempts to exercise his expertise.

Bill realized that he thrived in places where his area of expertise was respected and he was given a great deal of authority and autonomy to respond to situations quickly. Identification of job satisfiers and dissatisfiers helped him realize that he belonged back in the executive suite of a corporation.

Job Satisfiers and Dissatisfiers

Goals and skills begin to give your possibility form; satisfiers and dissatisfiers take the specificity, detail, and completeness to a new and essential level. Although the terminology is not as well known as skills and goals, the story of Bill demonstrates how essential the identification of satisfiers and dissatisfiers is to the process of translating possibilities into concrete targets.

Elements of fit and misfit with previous jobs and employers are critical data for creating a picture of the ideal job. An executive might enjoy planning and introducing new products and dislike jobs that involve maintaining the status quo. A lawyer might enjoy prosecuting white-collar crimes but dislike working in a small practice group where everyone is so specialized that there is little opportunity to work as a team. These details and the larger themes that emerge from the details are important building blocks in constructing a picture of a personally ideal job.

Specificity is essential to designing a career target. Make a specific and comprehensive list of job satisfiers and dissatisfiers. For example, listing "strategic planning" as one of your dislikes is too general. What is it about the process that you really dislike? The research? The writing? The financial analyses? The editing? Rewriting by others who want to control how the final plan reads rather than improving its quality?

Similarly, "sales" is too broad a category. What do you like best and least about sales: the identification of new markets, forming strategic partnerships, building sales teams, personally closing big deals, doing sales forecasts, exceeding sales quotas in tough competitive markets, rescuing the company from plummeting sales? Whatever the satisfier or dissatisfier, don't stop until you have articulated the most specific elements that were sources of great satisfaction or dissatisfaction.

Keep asking "What specifically did I like most about this?" until you can go no further. By gathering specific information you are building a picture of your personally ideal job, not some generic target. Copy and use the Satisfiers and Dissatisfiers Worksheet in Appendix F to record all your satisfiers and dissatisfiers. (Appendix A includes results from a completed example.)

Satisfiers and Dissatisfiers Worksheet

Analyze current and prior jobs carefully for the specific things you found particularly satisfying and dissatisfying. Although these factors are highly variable, the following questions may suggest some sources of satisfaction and dissatisfaction. There is no limit to the number of items you list. Use additional pages if necessary.

• What work interests you most and makes best use of your skills (specific projects, activities, organizational or job challenges)?

• What kinds of results are most meaningful to you?

• What roles do you enjoy most?

• What kinds of rewards matter most to you?

• What kind of people do you enjoy as colleagues and clients?

• What work setting is ideal?

• What is your preferred geographic location?

• What other factors have had a make-or-break impact on your satisfaction in each job?

This exercise looks in detail for information on which elements of work, environment, and context have been most important to you throughout your career. It draws on the information about goals and skills that you have already gathered. In addition, it incorporates information on interests, values, accomplishments, and needs or motivators, all of which define critical elements of personal career satisfaction.

Here are some questions to consider as you evaluate prior and current positions for satisfiers and dissatisfiers:

- What work interests you most and makes best use of your skills? What specific projects, activities, or organizational challenges have energized you most and made you happiest?

- What kinds of results are most meaningful to you? For example, do you derive your greatest satisfaction from creating something of your own, helping others, being recognized for your expertise, or something else?

- What roles do you enjoy most? Leader? Team member? Independent contributor? Expert? Project manager? People manager or coach? Consultant?

- What kinds of rewards matter most to you? Recognition from peers or supervisors? Stock options? Board exposure? Professional or industry visibility? Positive feedback? Salary? Task force assignments? Participation in Sloan Management or Harvard MBA Executive Programs or other educational or leadership opportunities?

- What kind of people do you enjoy as colleagues and clients? Ivy League graduates? International diplomats? Field reps who know the business from the ground up? An ethnically and educationally diverse group? What kind of person (education, background, training, etc.) or mix of people do you most enjoy?

- What work setting is ideal? This may include specific aspects of the corporate culture, working conditions, personal and professional development opportunities, or the preferred frequency and type of feedback.

- What is your preferred geographic location?
- What other factors have had a make-or-break impact on your satisfaction in each job?

By looking carefully for specific satisfiers and dissatisfiers in each position, you accumulate many building blocks to construct a picture of your ideal job. Maybe too many! The idea is to generate many factors, then narrow the list to a manageable few items. This process is the subject of the following section.

Narrowing the Factors

The next step is to narrow the list of satisfiers, skills, and goals and record these priority factors on the Ideal Job Factors Worksheet prior to rank ordering them. Prune the lengthy list of satisfiers and dissatisfiers by eliminating duplication, opposites of the same factor (e.g., a satisfier of *preparing financial reports* and a dissatisfier of *no financial report preparation*), and irrelevancies (such as *disliked working in Thailand* when you have no intention of working in Southeast Asia again, given your family situation). Look for headlines or main themes to trim the list prior to ranking the factors. When you have pruned the list, record up to 10 top satisfiers or dissatisfiers on the Ideal Job Factors Worksheet.

Also, list up to 5 of your greatest and most enjoyable skills from the Summary page of the Skills Inventory Worksheet and up to 4 priority goals from the Goal Planning Worksheet. (For additional guidance on this part of the process, refer to Appendix A.)

Now let's turn to how you can take the information you've gathered to find your own ideal job and inspiring career.

Ideal Job Factors Worksheet

Skills: What are your greatest and most enjoyable skills? List up to 5.

1.

2.

3.

4.

5.

Goals: What are your top career, relationship, and personal development goals? List up to 4.

1.

2.

3.

4.

Satisfiers and Dissatisfiers: What specific aspects of your job, work setting or culture, colleagues, or work situation are most satisfying and dissatisfying? List up to 10.

1.

2.

3.

4.

5.

6.

7.

8.

9.

10.

Ranking the Factors

Carefully completing the preceding exercises will generate a list of factors that specify your ideal job: your primary satisfiers and dissatisfiers and, to the extent that they were not identified in the satisfiers and dissatisfiers exercise, your priority goals and your greatest and most enjoyable skills. You already listed these factors on the Ideal Job Factors Worksheet.

The next step is to prioritize and reduce their number further, based on their relative importance to your career satisfaction. Use a simple forced-ranking technique to do so. Compare the first item on your list with every other item, assigning 1 point to the factor you consider more important to you. Compare the second item with all the remaining items, using the same process. Do this with every remaining item. The factor receiving the highest number of points scores at the top of the list. Use only the top 10 factors to specify your ideal job. Record these factors on the Ranked Ideal Job Factors Worksheet.

Five Straw Men

Consider how much of what appears on the final list of the top 10 factors is consistent with your current job. Clients often modify their initial stance of "anywhere but here, anything but this" once they have completed the assessment phase. Although some conclusions are dramatic (the lawyer turned actor, for example), there are usually some to many elements of the old in the picture of inspiring work. Reinvention may be total or partial, but clarifying or discovering what you love doing has a powerful impact.

The next step is to translate this information into real jobs using the straw men technique. This is a simple technique to move past the data gathering into imagining your future from the pieces of information you've gathered. This is where it's easy to get stuck. All of a sudden it's down to the wire: What is the ideal job? Many of my clients worry that they are about to draw the wrong conclusion with disastrous consequences.

Ranked Ideal Job Factors Worksheet

The Ideal Job Factors Worksheet lists up to 19 factors. Use the forced-ranking exercise to reduce and rank the total number of factors to no more than 10. Record those factors below, in order of importance.

To do this, compare each factor with all factors listed on the Ideal Job Factors Worksheet. Compare factor #1 with every other factor on your list. Which one is more important to you? Assign it a 1. Compare each factor with all the remaining factors.

Once you are done with this, take the second factor and compare it to the remaining factors on the list. Do the same comparisons with the third factor, and so on. When you are done, number the factors in descending order of importance, with the factor receiving the most votes of 1 at the top of the list. Record the top 10 factors below, with the top factor first.

Factor #1:

Factor #2:

Factor #3:

Factor #4:

Factor #5:

Factor #6:

Factor #7:

Factor #8:

Factor #9:

Factor #10:

The straw men technique is a way to get unstuck. How? Step outside yourself. Imagine that the major findings about you and your ideal job belong to someone else. Based on the priority factors listed in the Ranked Ideal Job Factors Worksheet, ask, What are up to five things this person could do? Use the answers to sketch pictures of at least three different positions.

Conduct a simple evaluation of how each alternative does or does not meet your top criteria. Nothing is perfect; even the ideal or perfect job has downsides and trade-offs. Use this technique to identify and compare the pluses and minuses of each potentially right job for you.

In some cases, you may not currently possess information to complete the evaluation. This will require talking to people in this job to find answers to questions. Use the Straw Men Worksheet to identify and evaluate these options.

Completing this exercise will provide you with an inspiring career possibility and target, an ideal job that incorporates and leverages your skills, accomplishments, values, interests, needs, and style. Later chapters show you how to create a resume to help you land that dream job.

Straw Men Worksheet

Review the following:

- The final set of priority factors or criteria from the self-assessment, as identified in the Ranking Ideal Job Factors Worksheet
- The career possibility you identified in the Possibilities chapter (Chapter 2)
- Any considerations from the Portfolio Career chapter (Chapter 5)

Pretend that you are an outside observer, reviewing this information about someone else. Identify up to five specific jobs that would be a great fit for this person. List them below. Complete a simple plus/minus evaluation of each job's fit with the priority job factors. Identify any missing information or gaps you need to address before you can complete the evaluation of this job.

Straw Man #1

- Job description

- Pluses
- Minuses
- Information gaps

Straw Man #2

- Job description

- Pluses
- Minuses
- Information gaps

Straw Men Worksheet (*Continued*)

Straw Man #3

- Job description

- Pluses
- Minuses
- Information gaps

Straw Man #4

- Job description

- Pluses
- Minuses
- Information gaps

Straw Man #5

- Job description

- Pluses
- Minuses
- Information gaps

Overall Evaluation and Selection of Alternatives

-
-
-
-

Chapter 5

The Portfolio of Career Skills
and Accomplishments

**Secret: A portfolio of career skills can advance your career
more than a traditional portfolio of positions.**

Skills, goals, and job satisfiers and dissatisfiers provide most of the
information to define the ideal job, but there's a final factor to consider. It has to do with the changing definition of careers. The portfolio career is defined by skills and accomplishments, not titles.
There are two major implications and uses of the portfolio career for
an executive wishing to make a move: one having to do with ex-
panding the potential targets for the right job, the other with precisely identifying the obstacles to the right job.

Employers and search consultants are generally looking to put
people into slots (or boxes) just like the ones they came from (or
fled). Viewing a portfolio career as the accumulation of portable
skills and marketable accomplishments that can be applied in many
settings expands the potential career choices. For an accomplished
executive looking to make a change, the portfolio career expands
the notion of what is possible beyond the past and into an arena as
vast as his or her skills and accomplishments without being limited
to jobs or titles just like previous ones.

Also, for many executives, the ideal job may be out of range for
the next job. Comparing your current portfolio of skills and accomplishments with the portfolio needed for the ideal job can identify
gaps that the next right move should fill to maximize your career
trajectory and ready yourself for the ideal job. Identifying the gaps

that stand between you and your ideal job enables you to make the wisest choice of next moves to accelerate progress to your ideal job.

Read the story of Susan for an example of how a portfolio career can expand your possibilities and move you into an exciting new position that is not necessarily on the identical path you were on. Appendix A provides another example.

The Importance of Portfolio Careers:
The Story of Susan

Susan was a CIO, a high-level technology leader with impressive achievements in some of the world's leading corporations. She had built world-class information technology organizations and teams, but when her position was eliminated following a merger, she used the downsizing as an opportunity to rethink her career direction. She loved the work but was burned out, exhausted, bored, and disillusioned by corporate politics. Although search consultants and employers pursued her with similar opportunities, Susan was interested in rethinking and reinventing her path.

What is the road map for this increasingly common situation? Susan used the portfolio career approach to identify the skills and accomplishments she had enjoyed most to define an ideal job consistent with her enthusiasm and her record. This meant leveraging her use of technology to increase productivity and profitability into a new direction where she could use her creativity but avoid the corporate bureaucracy.

In Susan's case, this meant joining a venture-capital-backed start-up that used technology to add value for consumers. Because technology was central to the company's value proposition, Susan could do what inspires her: building a company and team in a technology-driven company that makes a difference, not just a profit.

Susan's example shows the value of the portfolio career in clarifying ideal job targets. It demonstrates how a portfolio of highly marketable accomplishments and contributions can suggest a particular or alternative direction for turning your possibility into a job target. And it exemplifies how a portfolio of skills can do more to advance your career in the direction you want than a traditional portfolio of positions.

This is both a reasonability and a marketing check on your ideal job: What can you leverage best to define *and* land your ideal job? Although a portfolio career does not limit you to a traditional career path, it does require that you have the skills and accomplishments to do the job and to convince others you can do it, or it can highlight the skills you must acquire. You may aspire to be a yoga master, but don't expect anyone to hire you unless you have done the necessary work and have the track record to prove it.

The portfolio career is a useful tool for understanding your ideal job and making the right career moves toward or into it.

PREPARING THE TOOLS TO FIND THE RIGHT JOB

Career Tool 1: Resume

Chapter 6

The Resume as a Confidence Booster

Secret: The first reason to write a resume is to sell yourself to *you*.

A powerful resume is important whether or not you're actively seeking a job or promotion. If you're like most of my clients, you're approaching the topic of resumes with a mixture of dread and despair. You're probably looking for an out: "I haven't done a resume in 20 years" (the "too hard/too old" excuse); "I already have a resume—can't we just fix it?" (the "too lazy" excuse); "I'm not a great writer" (the "can't you do it for me?" excuse); or "I'm senior/well-known/visible enough that I don't need a resume" (the "too important" excuse). None of these excuses, or the many others I've heard, is sufficient justification for not preparing your resume.

Everyone needs a resume, regardless of situation, seniority, or stellar record. In fact, everyone needs a *great* resume, and it's worth every bit of effort, pain, and self-examination to produce one. If your success and happiness depended on a fantastic and unique product that was unknown, wouldn't you invest heavily in marketing it? *You* are that fantastic and unique product, and your resume is your most important marketing tool throughout your career.

51

Why Everyone Needs a Resume

Why go to the trouble of preparing a resume if you have no interest in changing jobs? Preparation for the unexpected is one reason. In today's volatile marketplace, things can change suddenly. Companies merge, are acquired, go bankrupt. Key players leave, and the scene or prospects change. Global competitors emerge. Scandals erupt. Terrorists strike. New opportunities suddenly arise. A long list of unexpected events and situations can precipitate a change of jobs. An up-to-date resume is part of an up-to-date career contingency plan. It's smart to have one.

A resume is also a useful tool for making a case for a promotion, an internal job change, assignment to a high-profile project or task force, a raise, or a board position. But its first use is as a source of self-confidence. Dr. Alan Weiss, the author of *Million Dollar Consulting* and other books on building and marketing your business, says, "The first sale is to yourself," emphasizing the critical importance of believing in your own worth as a contributor. In other words, a resume is a sales document, and the first sale is to yourself. Done right, the accomplishments in your resume should inspire your job search and other career-promoting efforts by building your own confidence so you can build others' confidence in you.

A resume is the best tool for this. Let me explain. I often give clients anonymous sample resumes from earlier clients to provide concrete examples. The universal reaction is intimidation. Clients conclude that they could never produce a comparably powerful resume. Ironically, the authors of the sample resumes had the same initial reaction to the sample resumes I showed them.

As one client said, "I look at my resume and I know everything in it is true, but I can't believe how good it sounds or how great it makes me feel reading it." The following chapters provide the rationale and step-by-step process necessary to produce a winning resume like his.

As a tool for self-marketing and self-examination, a resume can help you to succeed at:

- Landing a new job
- Securing a promotion, raise, or new assignment at your current job
- Uncovering experience or skill gaps that need to be filled through new assignments, new activities, or new jobs
- Identifying new opportunities or maximizing competitiveness for existing opportunities
- Competing for board, community, professional, industry, or trade positions
- Obtaining funding for a new venture
- Forming a career contingency plan if your job or company goes down the drain
- Building your self-confidence
- Clarifying long-term career targets and goals

See the Sample Chronological Resume for a complete example of this resume format. The resumes in Chapters 6 and 10 have been reduced to fit the smaller book pages, but your resume should be on 8½" × 11" paper.

The Importance of Being Prepared:
The Story of Larry

Larry called asking for urgent assistance. The top job managing the finance organization of the Fortune 50 investor-owned utility where he worked was open and he was interested. It was an entrée to deal with Wall Street and large institutional investors. It was an opportunity to lead a 150-person organization, twice the size of his current job. All in all, it was a significant step up, and he felt ready for the challenge.

The challenge he wasn't so sure about was his resume. He didn't have one. He recognized that wanting or needing a great resume in an instant is not the same as producing one. Could I help? Fortunately, I was available. But not everyone has a specialist to turn to.

Sample Chronological Resume

NAME

Home Address	Office: 212-555-5555
New York, NY 10021	Home: 212-333-3333
candidate@aol.com	Cell: 917-444-3333

CAREER SUMMARY

Operations executive and general manager with over 15 years of experience with Fortune 500 corporations in the financial services, technology, and media sectors. Demonstrated ability to turn around underperforming businesses and improve profitability through cost management, technology innovations, and reengineering employee work patterns.

PROFESSIONAL EXPERIENCE

1998 –
Present

NAME OF EMPLOYER New York, NY

President & General Manager, Middle Market Division
Manage all domestic and international middle-market activities for the fifth largest financial services company in the world. Full P&L responsibility for Finance, Credit, Operations, Sales, Marketing, MIS, Human Resources, and Legal functions. Responsible for 1,000 employees in the United States and $150M budget.

- Increased profits 29% by refocusing product lines and selling or closing three unprofitable businesses

- Reduced operating costs by $30M with no loss of productivity by consolidating six domestic profit centers and reducing senior management positions by 20%

- Grew earning assets from $3.0B to $3.7B in only four years

- Doubled the number of credit card orders processed daily by restructuring order processing system and providing the first intensive cross training to employees

1991 –
1998

NAME OF EMPLOYER New York, NY

Senior Vice President & General Manager (1996–1998)
Promoted from Vice President of Operations and Administration (1993–1996) and Operations Manager (1991–1993) to this position as chief operating officer of the largest division of this international media company. P&L responsibility for 200-person division with budget of $55M.

- Reversed a long-term volume decline and built gross revenues from $80M to over $125M in four years

- Created a profitable mail-order business that grew revenues to $15M within 24 months

- Improved unit volume of mature product line 30% through product quality upgrades and innovative web-based consumer promotions that became the industry standard

Sample Chronological Resume *(Continued)*

1987 – **NAME OF EMPLOYER** Palo Alto, CA
1991 Vice President, Administration & Operations (1988–1991)
Responsibility for day-to-day operations and finance, including budget preparation and
monitoring, and financial reporting for the business unit that accounts for 98% of company
revenues of this Fortune 100 high-tech manufacturer.

- Organized and directed project team that developed PC-based system to streamline
  billing process, reducing delinquent accounts by 20%

- Developed job rotation and training system that virtually eliminated management
  employee turnover for three years

- Redesigned worldwide consolidation processes, reducing closing time by 25%

Operations Manager (1987–1988)
Day-to-day management of operations and P&L responsibility for this $40M division,
with staff of 100.

- Uncovered $1M fraud that led to termination of senior operations managers and
  implementation of new financial and operating controls

- Saved $10M/year in rent through comprehensive companywide program of office
  relocation and consolidation

- Doubled revenues generated from middle-market business accounts by developing
  first cafeteria approach to account pricing

EDUCATION

1987 M.B.A. Harvard Business School, Cambridge, MA

1985 B.A. Political Science, with Highest Honors, Stanford University, Palo Alto, CA

PROFESSIONAL & COMMUNITY AFFILIATIONS

Member, Board of Directors of EastWest Industries & Junior Achievement of
Westchester County

And what followed was a frantic effort on our part to produce a resume and a stressful crash course in resume preparation.

A couple of weeks later, he called me, laughing. "Guess what the chairman said when he saw my resume?" I had no idea. "He was suspicious that I was looking for an outside job!" The vice chairman had to gently remind the chairman that he had encouraged the company's executives to prepare resumes as a way to compete for new jobs within the company, develop new skills, and increase their marketability. Larry got the job.

The point is this: You never know when you'll need a resume. Why not be prepared for the unexpected?

Chapter 7

Redefine Your Resume

Secret: A resume is not your career in the rearview mirror.

Definition and Purpose of a Resume

Contrary to traditional ideas about the resume as a record of work history, a resume is focused on the future, and where you're heading, not the past and what you've done. The traditional emphasis on job descriptions provides important information on the general scope of responsibility, but a resume is *not* simply or primarily a record of previous jobs and employers. The longer your career, the more important your track record is relative to job scope, prestige of employers, or educational institutions. Accomplishments, not job descriptions, are the centerpiece of a strong resume.

Because the best predictor of future performance is past performance, the focus should be on performance and results. Accomplishments—specific contributions or actions with quantified results or benefits—are the bricks and mortar of a strong case. They can market you in a way that job descriptions alone can't. See Differentiating Job Descriptions from Accomplishments for examples that differentiate the two.

Differentiating Job Descriptions from Accomplishments

Some job seekers use the same bulleted format for job descriptions and accomplishments, confusing the prospective employer and presenting a disorganized, incoherent case for their candidacy.

Test your understanding of the differences by distinguishing the accomplishments from the job descriptions in the following examples. (Hint: accomplishments are specific and quantified; job descriptions refer to scope of responsibility. The answers are provided after the examples.)

An Example for Executives

1. Managed all aspects of an aggressive two-year growth plan
2. Oversaw all administrative departments, including finance and accounting, facilities, MIS, and human resources
3. Built new department in 90 days that processes 35,000 claims a month, 15 percent more than the industry standard
4. Spearheaded acquisition of $50M annual revenue hospital that increased market share by 15 percent
5. Established and managed regional services for $300M region of Fortune 500 health care chain

An Example for Lawyers

1. Negotiated and closed transactions, including loan workouts, restructuring, lender liability claims, and foreclosures
2. Drafted sophisticated antitakeover measures as part of $300M merger of two publicly held Internet companies
3. Participated in legal due diligence for corporate acquisitions in 10 Western states; handled mergers among subsidiaries; prepared resolutions and other corporate documents
4. Structured $10M joint venture between U.S. biotechnology company and European pharmaceutical conglomerate that led to the development of the first AIDS vaccine
5. Developed standard documents for companywide commercial real estate lending program with an estimated $3B portfolio

(continued)

Answers

- *For executive example:* (1), (2), and (5) are job descriptions; (3) and (4) are specific accomplishments.
- *For lawyer example:* (1), (3), and (5) are job descriptions; (2) and (4) are specific accomplishments.

Why Accomplishments Matter: The Story of Katherine

Katherine is one of those smart, creative marketing executives who seems able to do it all. She has worked for some of the top companies in retail, media, technology, and consumer products, as well as the leading advertising agencies. You may not know Katherine, but you know her work, from a famous athletic shoe ad to a campaign that catapulted a top PC manufacturer from being a niche player to one of a handful of credible brand choices.

Recently, Katherine got a call from her favorite client, the CEO of a media start-up. Katherine loves media, loves start-ups, loves the players in this company. She's aligned with its marketing strategy, which she largely authored. The CEO was ready to hire a vice president of marketing. He encouraged her to apply but warned her that the company needed to go through a formal search.

We started with an old resume long on job descriptions and details and short on contributions and quantified results. The first accomplishment on her resume was "Responsible for all business aspects of this brand and marketing consulting company, including business development, client relations, and day-to-day operations; business was conceived and grown in the worst economic climate in years."

The first accomplishment in the final version was "Evolved Company X's brand positioning and developed a brand campaign that increased viewers by 70 percent." Outstanding as she was, her old resume, which focused on job descriptions, would have made it hard for her client to hire her. Her new resume, which focused on accomplishments, made it easy.

Refer to How Accomplishments Build a Case to assist you further in constructing your most powerful resume.

How Accomplishments Build a Case

One of the clearest ways to demonstrate how accomplishments can build a case is to compare two different cases for the position of chief financial officer. For example:

1. An **operations-type CFO** built his case by emphasizing accomplishments that underline success in making better use of people and equipment:

   - Increased net income by $10M by introducing a pay-for-performance plan and creating an inventory management system
   - Saved $5M in software development costs by designing budgeting and internal reporting models that were sought by competitors for purchase
   - Initiated annual savings of $100M by negotiating more favorable interest rates with five different financial institutions

   These accomplishments build the case for this executive's ability to enhance profitability by identifying and implementing operating efficiencies.

2. A **fund-raising CFO** would pursue a different kind of CFO job and emphasize accomplishments that show extensive public markets experience and investment background and contacts for different sources of funding, such as:

   - Managed 10 initial and secondary public securities offerings, which raised $900 million
   - Led contract negotiations and due diligence for merger with $250 million NYSE professional services company
   - Raised $200 million in financing through accounts receivable securitization program

Chapter 8

Three Approaches to Accomplishments

**Secret: A triage approach will generate
the best set of accomplishments.**

Preparing to Write Your Resume

Before you begin writing your resume, you have four important things to do:

1. Gather career information.
2. Define your accomplishments.
3. Refine and quantify your accomplishments.
4. Decide on the resume format.

This chapter focuses on Steps 1 and 2. Step 3 is covered in Chapter 9; Step 4 is covered in Chapter 10.

Gather Career Information

To facilitate the resume writing process, begin by collecting data about job titles, years of employment, employers, educational institutions, degrees, and credentials, along with performance reviews. Collect old resumes and deal sheets, your corporate or firm bio, as well as any other pertinent information.

Define Your Accomplishments

A resume needs to highlight a combination of achievements that conveys your unique style, personality, and contributions. A subjective list of adjectives or standard job descriptions won't do this. Accomplishments will.

Accomplishments reveal and demonstrate your skills, identify results and outcomes, and prepare you for the interview. Trying to weasel out of the important, though tedious, work of describing accomplishments is a mistake. My clients have been known to adopt the language and achievements of sample resumes I provide for them. They don't get away with it. Shortcutting the process or relying only on past performance reviews or old resumes cheats no one but you.

You can generate the best and most comprehensive set of accomplishments by using all of the following three approaches:

1. Greatest accomplishments
2. Skill-based accomplishments
3. Expertise-based accomplishments

Most people use only the first strategy, but using all three and triangulating among them will produce the best results.

Greatest Accomplishments

Make a list of your most significant accomplishments. Think back over your career at the achievements that stand out, such as:

- Landed an unlandable deal
- Resolved a costly conflict between your company and a competitor
- Won a case against all odds
- Produced an award-winning advertising campaign
- Guided the restructuring of stock option plans
- Cut operating costs by 20 percent

What achievements made you proudest? What contributions received the most recognition? What results do people still talk about? Remember that your greatest accomplishments don't necessarily reflect where you spent the most time, nor are they necessarily the most recent. What they should do is represent where you have made the greatest contribution.

To jog your memory, think about people you've worked with, positions you've held, events, awards, and so on. If you need additional inspiration, consult performance reviews, colleagues, bosses, maybe even a proud parent.

Skill-Based Accomplishments

Once you've listed your greatest accomplishments, identify your greatest skills, strengths, and areas of knowledge, using information from the Skills Inventory Worksheet that you completed in Chapter 4. Some or all of your greatest and most enjoyed skills should be the basis for accomplishment statements.

Accomplishments representing a specific instance in which you used one of your greatest and most enjoyed skills to produce a measurable result belong on your resume. Suppose that negotiating is a highly developed skill of yours and one you enjoy using a great deal. Think of a specific instance in which your negotiating skill led to a measurable result.

For example, consider the time you managed to resolve a problem with an outstanding bill without losing either the money or the client. Or perhaps you enjoy finding faster ways to do things and do this especially well. Remember the time you devised a quick solution to a client's last-minute request prior to a trade show or a court appearance?

If there's no overlap between the accomplishments on your resume and your greatest and most enjoyed skills, then you're building a case for a job you don't want. Things you do well, but hate doing, don't belong in your resume.

Expertise-Based Accomplishments

This approach uses important categories of expertise for your target job to generate accomplishments. Put yourself in the shoes of a prospective employer looking to hire someone for your target job. In what areas would he or she reasonably expect to see accomplishments? These might be:

- Functional—for example, a chief operating officer might have experience (and accomplishments) in MIS, accounting, and facilities; an intellectual property lawyer might have expertise in trademark, patents, and copyrights.
- Experience with a kind of situation or project—such as layoffs, M&A, jury trial, high growth, IPO, or managing people.
- General expertise useful for virtually any position—such as cost-cutting or customer/client service.

Use the areas of expertise for the job you want as a template of what an employer needs. As you write your accomplishment list, check to see where there's under- or overcoverage according to the template. Do you have three cost-cutting accomplishments, four information technology accomplishments, and no people or project management accomplishments? Use the template to identify gaps and generate new accomplishments to fill them, to make needed changes in emphasis, or to eliminate redundancies. This approach is the least familiar but potentially the most important, so don't overlook it.

Chapter 9

Maximize Accomplishment Impact

Secret: Less is more when it comes to accomplishments.

The next step has two parts: refining achievements in accomplishment form, then quantifying them for maximum impact.

Refine Your Accomplishments

Accomplishments are achievements or results of your work. Well-formulated accomplishments have two parts: what you actually accomplished and the measurement or benefit. A good accomplishment is a sentence-long bullet, usually of no more than two lines (but often three lines in the smaller format of this book), beginning with a strong verb that describes a specific contribution and its quantified results. To enhance readability, precede and follow the statement with a double space.

A few words about brevity of accomplishments. Most of my clients find brevity a particularly difficult objective to achieve. Their detailed knowledge of just how difficult it was to produce certain results makes it very hard for them to part with all the detail in their accomplishment statements. Yet, when it comes to the length of accomplishments, less is often more. Let me share an example.

One day, while teaching a resume seminar for an international career consulting firm, I made a point about how paragraphs often masquerade as bullets. To illustrate, I used the following accomplishment: "Improved forms and procedures for opening new accounts by developing a universal signature card that replaced 14 separate forms, reduced printing and inventory expenses, and enhanced customer service by saving account opening time."

Enough already! This bullet is overly detailed, with too many results and not enough quantification. It exemplifies trying to do too much using too many words. Here's my proposed replacement: "Developed a universal signature card that replaced 14 separate forms and cut account opening time by 30 percent." This bullet is less than half the length and has twice the impact because it highlights and quantifies the most important results. Strive for brevity as you refine your accomplishments.

Check Appendix B for a list of action verbs to start your accomplishments and to remind yourself of different kinds of accomplishments.

Quantify Your Accomplishments

Quantification is a new and unfamiliar way of looking at your achievements, a new language. It takes time to master, but it is worth the effort in terms of impact. Every single client of mine has pointed out how his or her job doesn't lend itself to quantification. I point right back to my experience that, with effort and ingenuity, almost every accomplishment can be quantified. When you think of quantification, you might immediately think of making money. Dollars, percentages, and speed are common metrics, but by no means the only ones.

Measurable results can take many other forms, such as:

- Saving money or time
- Reducing errors
- Increasing profits, revenues, or market share
- Cutting staff
- Improving quality, service, teamwork, or morale
- Decreasing turnover, absenteeism, or customer complaints
- Achieving the same results with fewer resources
- Achieving more with the same resources

- Improving operations or making things easier, better, or faster
- Doing something for the first time, particularly if it's adopted by others
- Resolving a crisis or problem with little or no increase in time, dollars, energy, people, and so on

Accomplishments are usually strongest when they reference one particular incident, but sometimes the sheer number of times you've done something, or the sheer size of the project, can be sufficient. For example, when a client was in the process of making a transition from lawyer to law school professor, we quantified the number of motions she had argued to show the level of her presentation skills. Another client touted the high number of major system installations he had directed successfully as a way of reinforcing his IT expertise.

Compare the following:

- Represented major investment banker in public offerings and private placements

with

- Represented underwriters and issuers in over 40 public debt and equity securities offerings totaling $2.3 billion

Or compare:

- Implemented major corporate initiative on productivity

with

- Saved $19M in year one by introducing work simplification and employee decision-making procedures as part of a productivity initiative

Although quantification is desirable, sometimes it's not possible. Accomplishments that reflect contributions to a bet-the-company project or writing a brief that became the basis of a new law exemplify important contributions that cannot be quantified but should be included in your resume.

Chapter 10

Pick the Best Resume Format

Secret: Resume format is a marketing decision.

Although accomplishments are the centerpiece of your resume, format increases the marketing impact. Here, you have three choices:

1. *Chronological:* A chronological format presents job descriptions and accomplishments associated with each job. This is the standard resume format. Employers and search consultants expect it and are comfortable with it. Refer back to the sample chronological resume in Chapter 6 for an example. This format has the greatest marketing impact and is the one to use unless you're considering a dramatic change in the direction of your career or employment, in which case a representative accomplishments format may be preferable.

2. *Functional:* A functional format presents accomplishments associated with skills or functional categories, not with jobs. Sales, marketing, and change management are examples. From a marketing standpoint, a functional resume has two major disadvantages. First, a resume with an alternative format can create suspicion: What's he or she trying to hide? Most employers and search consultants dislike functional resumes.

Second, the functional categories you select aren't necessarily the most meaningful ones to your prospective employer. You wouldn't market a great product in a package that customers hate, so why make that mistake with your resume format?

3. *Representative accomplishments:* Spent your career in one organization? Many employers automatically view you as a one-trick pony or a one-company person. Spent the past 10 years in development at a major nonprofit but want to move to a sales position in business? Many business employers will reject you as a nonprofit type. Want a job that capitalizes on the analytical work you did early in your career? Employers will discount this experience as out of date. Spent your career in a big law firm but want to move to a smaller boutique? Smaller firms may fear that you have big firm requirements for support staff and other resources.

A representative accomplishments format emphasizes what you've done, rather than where or when you did it. It does this by putting accomplishments at the beginning of the resume, immediately after the Career Summary and before the Professional Experience/Work History section, rather than with the jobs on which they occurred.

This is helpful when you're changing:

- Industries or functions
- Companies after many years or an entire career with one employer
- Focus within an industry or function

See the Sample Representative Accomplishments Resume for an example. This corporate securities partner from a big law firm was seeking a position in a corporation or with another law firm after many years with one firm. He was an excellent lawyer with top technical and client service skills, someone who worked at a high level of proficiency and speed.

Why would he have any trouble making the desired move? For law firms, he lacked the sizable portable book of business that most firms require of partners. For corporations, his long tenure with a firm might raise questions about the depth of people and organizational leadership they needed for a general counsel, as he was far too senior for a junior in-house role.

Sample Representative Accomplishments Resume

NAME
700 Park Avenue
New York, NY 10021
212-555-5515 (H)
212-555-5516 (F)
917-319-5515 (Cell)
Name@gmail.com

CAREER SUMMARY

Corporate attorney with 20+ years of broad experience in Wall Street private practice with particular expertise in corporate finance and securities. Career focus on structuring complex transactions using innovative and streamlined approaches that have become the industry standard. Recognized within the firm and industry for outstanding client service and associate development skills. Selected as one of the Best Lawyers in America for past 10 years.

REPRESENTATIVE ACCOMPLISHMENTS

- Managed over 35 public and private securities offerings, involving $2B of debt and equity securities

- Orchestrated 20 mergers and acquisitions ranging in size from $300M to $1.5B

- Created a tax-advantaged structure for a $300M cross-border gas pipeline

- Structured $500M debt and equity investment in national hardware chain, including $100M franchisee asset purchase and $75M bank loan

- Led a $200M roll-up of 30 tax shelter partnerships into a newly formed corporation

- Assumed control of and successfully completed a $75M public offering on one day's notice when colleague underwent medical emergency

- Designed joint venture for U.S. manufacturer and Chinese conglomerate, with $20M private equity investment, $15M credit extension, and Asian product distribution rights

- Successfully completed a $200M initial public offering for an international biotech company

- Structured sophisticated antitakeover measures as part of a $1B merger of two publicly held software companies

- Completed the amicable termination of a $1M facilities management contract within two weeks after months of unsuccessful attempts by client

- Drafted first cobranding agreement that served as national model for major multimedia firm

- Managed 20-person cross-office teams preparing series of 50 matters in one year for Fortune 20 securities firm as part of a successful divestiture

- Selected to chair Lateral Partner Integration Committee

(continued)

Sample Representative Accomplishments Resume *(Continued)*

WORK HISTORY

1980 –   **NAME OF FIRM**   New York, NY/Washington, DC
Present

Partner: 1988–Present

Associate: 1980–1988

Elected to partner (1988) from associate for this 1,000-attorney full-service law firm with 15 offices worldwide. General corporate practice counseling public and private companies on a wide variety of corporate matters, including financings, mergers and acquisitions, corporate formation, and complex restructuring/recapitalization.

EDUCATION and BAR ADMISSIONS

1979   JD, Columbia University, New York, NY

1976   BA, Psychology & BA, History, Georgetown University, Washington, DC
            Phi Beta Kappa

            Admitted to the District of Columbia (1980) and New York State (1981) Bars

PROFESSIONAL & COMMUNITY AFFILIATIONS

Board of Directors, Mechanics Bank

Board of Directors, New York City Chapter of Junior Achievement

Executive Committee Member, NYC Bar Association Committee to Rebuild Ground Zero

Junior Warden of the Vestry, St. Bartholomew's Church

He was trying to do several things by using this resume format: de-emphasize a career with a single employer; highlight technical skills through the complexity, frequency, and variety of transactions he had handled; and showcase his people management and firm and civic leadership track record.

Note how the format reinforces the paramount importance of accomplishments: Because the first page is limited to the Career Summary and Representative Accomplishments (this section can also be labeled "Selected Accomplishments" or "Key Accomplishments"), the reader's attention is captured by contributions and results, is not diverted by positions or employers, and does not have dates to suggest length of tenure or age. Although the first page does not always exclude the experience section, it often does in a lengthy career.

Chapter 11

Optimize Resume Length

Secret: There's a winning length for a resume.

What's the appropriate length of a resume, from a marketing standpoint? Perhaps no other issue has caused more debate. Some advocate a one-page resume, but how can you condense 10, 20, or 30+ years of a career into one page? It's a marketing impossibility. There just isn't sufficient space for your most impressive accomplishments, along with job descriptions and information on employers. Unless you've had only one job, it's likely that you'll undermine your marketing message. And resorting to small font sizes, tiny margins, and dense fields of text fails the test of readability.

On the other side are those who contend that a resume should document your career exhaustively, regardless of length. This perspective is rooted in the practices of executive search consultants hired by companies to identify qualified potential candidates. Once the search firm has narrowed the pool, it repackages their resumes into lengthy narratives and presents them to the client company. This is a special case in which the use of long resumes is expected, but it in no way supports their general use.

When it comes to using a resume as a marketing tool, limiting it to no more than two pages is essential. Employers don't have the time or the desire to read more. Your most readable resume will use a 12-point font size, one-inch margins, and plenty of double spaces, including between bullets.

Your ability to limit yourself to two pages implies that you're bottom-line-oriented. Is there an employer who's not seeking a strong bottom-line orientation? By the time you reach the executive ranks, a strong presentation of your track record will require two pages. Make those two pages count.

Chapter 12

The Myth of Multiple Resumes

Secret: Don't customize resumes to a job or employer.

The idea that you need multiple versions of your resume to sell yourself most effectively to prospective employers is a myth and a mistake.

Multiple resumes are generally of two forms:

1. The same resume with a different job objective
2. A resume written expressly for a particular job

Changing only the objective is a bad idea for a few reasons. A job objective is generally not part of an executive resume. Tacking a different objective on the same resume hardly constitutes building a strong case for a different job. Finally, the "wrong" resume can fall into the hands of the "right" person in the course of your networking activities.

If you fear that a single resume limits the potential scope of your opportunities, consider two things. First, as an executive with a substantial track record, rather than a junior employee at the start of a career, it's unlikely that you can build a powerful case in wildly different directions.

Second, executives frequently face the challenge of seniority, particularly when they're changing direction. Prospective employers often prefer to go with the more junior candidate (read: cheaper and more malleable), particularly from the same industry and function. An executive candidate needs to build a com-

74

pelling case that his or her seniority and seasoning have produced measurable and relevant results for an employer. It's unlikely that you can build strong multiple cases.

If you can do so, pursue the different directions sequentially rather than simultaneously. Pick the direction that best fits your ideal job target, construct your strongest resume, and set a time limit for the search. If you don't turn up opportunities within this period, prepare the strongest resume for your second direction.

There's a much more efficient and effective way to customize your approach to a particular employer or opportunity—competitive advantages—which we'll cover in later chapters.

Chapter 13

Optimize Resume Structure

Secret: Resume impact isn't solely determined by content.

Drafting Your Resume

A winning resume generally includes the following components:

- Streamlined, chronological format
- Career summary that makes a strong first impression
- Brief, selective, and employer-focused presentation of job responsibilities and results
- Quantified accomplishments that make an employer take notice

This chapter shows how to draft and optimize each component of resume structure (except for the Career Summary, which is covered in the next chapter) so you can make the most of your resume as a sales and marketing document. The back of the book contains additional resources to help you prepare your resume: Sample Accomplishments, with numerous examples organized by different jobs, functions, and industries are included in Appendix C. Appendix D, About the Resume, contains Resume Dos and Don'ts for things to include and avoid in creating a powerful resume; Top 10 Executive Resume Mistakes; and Guide to a Winning Resume, which summarizes the entire resume process.

After you've generated your initial list of accomplishments, the next step is to put together the basic structure of your resume:

- Identifying Information
- Career Summary
- Professional Experience or Work History
- Education
- Professional and Community Affiliations

Each of these components is addressed in the following sections. Career Summary is discussed in Chapter 14, as that's the final section written. The following discussion assumes that you're using the standard chronological format.

Identifying Information

Basic identifying information, including name, home address, home and work phone numbers, e-mail address, and fax and cell phone numbers, belongs at the top of your resume. The format you choose for this header is up to you. Avoid using a larger font for your name and address, unusual graphics or design, or any other gimmicks. You're an executive, not an artist. Let your accomplishments attract the attention.

Professional Experience

The next section, Professional Experience or Work History (select the combination of words you prefer to title this section), presents work experience in reverse chronological order. Include the past 10 or 15 years of work experience; additional jobs are optional. No matter how far back you go, remember to emphasize those positions that are relevant to building the case for your target job. If you held a job in an unrelated field, omit or de-emphasize it.

The basic information on each job (title, employer, location, and years of employment) is followed by a brief paragraph describing the job and then a set of bullets listing major accomplishments in that job. Keep it short—employers will hire you more for your achievements than your responsibilities.

Job description should include your scope of responsibility, including P&L responsibility, if any, size of staff and budget, functional or other major responsibilities, and unique components (such as a CFO who also manages MIS and HR). Include a few words about the employer in the strongest terms possible (e.g., "a Fortune 500 high-tech manufacturer," "one of the top 25 law firms in the United States," "a $1B electronic game software company," or "the leading online retailer").

Avoid company or industry jargon. This requires vigilance. It's easy to become so used to certain terms that you forget that they don't have universal meaning. Jargon can create unintended barriers. For example, say "managed project teams," not "managed client engagement teams," if you are seeking a corporate job, not a public accounting job.

Select accomplishments from the list you developed and place them under the appropriate job, in order of importance. In other words, if a prospective employer could know only one thing you had accomplished at a job, what would it be? If only two things, what would they be? And so on. There's no right number of accomplishments per job. However, employers generally expect to see more accomplishments in your most recent, and presumably most senior, positions. See Professional Experience/Work History for examples of this section.

Education

Complete the Education section, listing dates, degrees, field or major, institutions, and locations. Place the most recent degree first. Don't pad with in-house or outside seminars unless they have substantive relevance to the case you're building. Include credentials if you have them, such as CPA or Bar admissions.

Professional and Community Affiliations

Affiliations are important only if you occupied board or other leadership positions, membership itself was an honor, your membership alone is an asset to a prospective employer, or they're central to your case. Omit them otherwise.

Professional Experience/Work History

Example 1:

PROFESSIONAL EXPERIENCE

1985 –   **BIG LAW FIRM**   San Francisco, CA
1996   Administrator
Managed operations and staffing functions for this general service 300-attorney law firm with offices in San Francisco, New York City, and Chicago. Oversight responsibility for finance and accounting, MIS, human resources, business services, and facilities. Supervised staff of 15 and operating budget of $30M.

- Established the firm's first collection department that reduced accounts receivable over 90 days by 50% in the first year

- Introduced first performance-based compensation system that reduced turnover of top performers by 80% firmwide

- Coordinated a major demolition and construction project in only 2.5 weeks, so that scheduled move and new subtenant occupancy occurred on time

Example 2:

WORK HISTORY

1990 –   **GUARDIAN INC.**   New York, NY
2000   President and General Manager – Equipment Financing
Turned around and managed equipment financing division of world's largest financial services conglomerate. Full P&L responsibility for Finance, Credit, Operations, Sales, Marketing, Systems, and Legal functions. Responsible for 3,000 employees worldwide and $250M expense budget.

- Increased profits 30% to $35M and doubled return on equity to 15%

- Reduced 60+ day delinquencies by over 50% within first six months

- Reorganized and consolidated five domestic profit centers, reducing annual operating costs by 25%

For example, I worked with a client looking for CFO jobs. The affiliations section of her resume listed the California Female CPA Association. I asked her, "Who belongs to this association? Is it by invitation only?" She answered that the membership included female CPAs in the state. In that case, I recommended she list CPA under the Education section of her resume, but omit the CPA association from the list of affiliations.

On the other hand, I worked with a bank president who had a long list of professional and community affiliations. Some were in board or other leadership positions, others were not. However, we included all of them in his resume. Why? Because part of what an employer is "buying" in a bank president is his or her involvement in the community.

Finishing Your Resume

There are just two more things to do to convert your draft resume into the finished document you want to show the world: Polish your accomplishments and write your career summary.

Polish Your Accomplishments

Defining accomplishments is a process that takes some time. Honing your list of accomplishments and clarifying how each is expressed should continue as you write and edit your resume.

To be honest, my clients generally hate this process; they think I'm deranged because I relish it. But I know that the shaping and sculpting of accomplishments is an art that produces great results with search consultants and employers.

As an example, a client of mine, an expert in corporate governance, had several corporate governance accomplishments referring to his involvement in the board recruitment and training process. An earlier version of his resume included:

- Implemented new board priorities and staff
- Designed and led the first board and senior management training in corporate governance for nonprofits

These accomplishments were wan—colorless, generic, uninteresting, totally unlike him. I raised the "So what?" veto. What was the result of the new priorities or the training? What concrete difference had they made?

He then realized that the net result had been to allow the board to go from an almost complete focus on short-term crises to a consideration of long-range issues. We finally created an accomplishment statement with real impact:

- Introduced corporate governance training that increased board time spent on long-term strategic priorities by 75 percent

This process not only improves the final resume, but it clarifies precisely what you're good at and what unique difference you've made. This clarification yields huge dividends in the networking and interview processes, where your success hinges on articulating what you want to do and why you're uniquely well qualified to do it. Refer to The Evolution of Accomplishments for examples.

The accomplishment-polishing process continues until the resume is in its final form. Look again at the mix of accomplishments, their content, language, syntax, and results. Make sure they represent your personality, style, and contributions. Should some be strengthened or eliminated? Do too many take the form of X resulting in Y, such as "Streamlined the proposal creation process, resulting in 20 percent increase in revenues year one"? When you don't diversify the way your accomplishments are stated, the rhythm will lull an employer to sleep!

To facilitate creating future resumes, keep a log to record accomplishments as they occur. The log provides useful information for salary and promotion negotiations, discussions about possible new assignments, and periodic reevaluations of your career plan. Recent accomplishments serve to measure your progress in developing your skills and career from year to year.

The Evolution of Accomplishments

The following examples illustrate that developing accomplishments is an iterative process.

Before	After
• Created and staffed the company's first self-directed work team	• Created and staffed the company's first self-directed work team that reduced supervisory staff 15% with no loss in productivity
• Developed and directed the strategic market plan opposing a proposed $300M pipeline expansion	• Saved $200M in construction costs for an unnecessary facility expansion project by developing a plan to optimize use of existing facilities
• Handled legal work on equity plans of public company to resolve shareholder approval issues	• Guided restructuring of stock option plans of $1B software company to resolve shareholder approval issues
(This is an example of focusing on different, stronger efficiency initiatives.) • Saved the company over $5,000 annually by automating all basic accounting functions, such as journal entries and statement of cash flows	• Organized and led project team that developed PC-based system to bill $3B annually of previously unbilled major accounts
• Created corporate governance structure for national roll-up transaction to enable efficient management of new entity while providing for balanced distribution of power, thus eliminating roadblocks to deal	• Eliminated roadblocks to $900M merger of six companies by creating a corporate governance structure providing for balanced distribution of power
• Sold to Fortune 100 companies	• Generated over $6M in annual sales to Fortune 100 companies, consistently winning awards for top 2% of account executives for 10 years

Chapter 14

The Importance of a Career Summary

Secret: The career summary is the executive summary of your career.

Properly constructed, the career summary presents your major qualifications to create a strong and immediate first impression on prospective employers. An effective career summary is the sharp edge of your marketing tool, yet most resumes overlook it. Don't make that mistake.

Though it starts your resume, write it last, once you've finalized the rest of the text. Otherwise, you're attempting the nearly impossible task of summarizing what doesn't yet exist.

The format of this section—one or two short paragraphs, a short paragraph and bullets, or all bullets—is secondary. The best format depends on the message you want to deliver. Tell a story; don't just list one sentence after another. Appropriate information for a career summary may include the following:

- Years of experience
- Kind of employer (industry, size, or growth stage), if appropriate
- Functional breadth
- Areas of particular expertise, demonstrated ability, or extensive experience
- Career focus, results, or track record (looking for themes that characterize your career)

Include any skills and knowledge important to the case you're building so that an employer doesn't overlook them. Do you have facility with a particular budget forecasting model, or with foreign or computer languages or software that is essential for your target position? Include unusual and advantageous degrees, such as a sales executive with an engineering degree looking for a job in high tech, a lawyer with an MBA looking to work in a corporate setting, or a COO with a PhD in biochemistry seeking work in a biotech. Or perhaps you have reached an exceptional level of professional excellence, as signified by an AV rating by Martindale-Hubbell for lawyers in a small firm or being included in the Best Lawyers in America if you're from a bigger firm (where AV ratings are standard). All of these are legitimate and powerful pieces of information for your career summary.

Tempting as it may be to describe your performance with adjectives like "organized," "dedicated," "hands-on," don't do it, even if they're true! They simply declare value without demonstrating it because they don't refer to objective areas of achievement. They take up space that can be used more effectively.

For example, compare the impact of the following two career summaries:

- Focused, dedicated, and results-oriented human resources executive with over 15 years of experience in Fortune 500 companies in high technology and health care sectors. Excellent organizational and team-building skills.

with

- Human resources executive with over 15 years of experience building customer-focused cultures in Fortune 500 companies in high technology and health care sectors. Experienced in establishing recruitment and retention programs that produced high levels of productivity and minimized attrition in key hires throughout major business changes such as mergers, restructurings, and international expansions.

The first example merely claims positive results, whereas the second demonstrates them objectively and more powerfully. Just as accomplishments go beyond job descriptions to show what you've done, a well-written career summary goes beyond particular jobs to show the results and expertise you've developed throughout your career.

Career Tool 2: Competitive Advantages

Chapter 15

Introducing Competitive Advantages

Secret: The success of your job search depends on the answer to "Why hire you?"

Strategic marketing and positioning are essential to leveraging your professional assets into a new position. Resumes are the first essential tool, competitive advantages the second. A resume builds your strongest case for employers or opportunities *in general*. Competitive advantages take case building to the next level by creating the strongest case *for a particular employer* or *opportunity*.

A successful job search depends on your ability to formulate a compelling answer to the fundamental question: Why hire *you*? Competitive advantages provide that answer.

Chapter 7 introduced accomplishments, statements of the specific and quantified contributions or achievements that form the heart of your resume and brand. Competitive advantages define your brand further through themes about your distinctive experience and achievements that build and customize your case. They draw explicit and factual links between the needs of an employer, assignment, job, or challenge, and your skills and experience. They demonstrate your value potential to a prospective employer in the strongest terms.

Competitive advantages make a powerful case. How? They tie together information from several accomplishments into broader factual themes. They may introduce information not in your resume but of significance to a particular employer. They are typically at a higher level of generality or abstraction than accomplishments. As such, they become the main points in the case you're building, with accomplishments the supporting evidence.

Competitive advantages are objective and specific and, whenever possible, quantified. They describe broader career themes or qualifications than a single accomplishment. "A track record of increasing sales by 30 percent or more in every prior position within the first year" is one example.

Resumes and Competitive Advantages

A resume summarizes and markets your case for your target audience in general. Because it should be no more than two pages, information that might be of particular significance to certain members of your target audience is left out in favor of information important to most. Competitive advantages, described in a cover letter or an interview, customize your resume so that you:

- Market yourself with the greatest impact by demonstrating your value potential for an employer and position
- Convey interest to your target audience in this *specific* opportunity, not just in any opportunity
- Demonstrate initiative in having learned about their needs and having built a specific case

It's theoretically possible to customize each resume you send out instead of using competitive advantages, but why do so? Competitive advantages save time and effort and increase the impact of your customization efforts, as you'll soon see. They help you write cover letters and provide data for your interviews and networking conversations.

Competitive advantages nail the fundamental job search question—Why hire you?—by making your competitive edge specific, measurable, explicit, and relevant to a specific opportunity and employer.

Chapter 16

How and Why Competitive
Advantages Work

Secret: It all comes down to *market*ability, not just ability.

Don't assume that having the skills and intelligence to do a dream job is enough for a successful search. It's not about whether you can *do* the job, it's about whether someone will *hire* you to do the job. This is *show*, not *tell*. You must demonstrate your ability to do the job by drawing specific factual links between what an employer needs and what you've already done. A successful job search requires marketing yourself explicitly and powerfully. Competitive advantages show your edge.

How Competitive Advantages Work:
The Story of Diane

Diane had spent her career in a Fortune 20 corporation. After 25 years, the thrill was gone, but the glass ceiling wasn't. For the first time in a long time, she felt excited when she heard about an opening for head of executive education at a top business school.

There was just one tiny hitch: She had no experience in university administration, much less executive education. How could Diane hope to win her dream job, competing against a host of directors of executive education programs at the country's leading business schools?

Had she adopted the strategy that job seekers and career reinventors generally recommend, she would have written a letter

89

pointing out to the search committee that she had 25 years of successful business experience and excellent interpersonal, communication, and management skills. Though true, this letter would have gone straight to the circular file. It just wouldn't be compelling enough to get an interview, much less a job, especially as a dark horse candidate.

Instead, she used competitive advantages to build the strongest factual case she could for her candidacy by demonstrating that her unique combination of capabilities and experience made her the best choice. Here are the main points we developed to present her case in the cover letter for her resume:

- Experience organizing successful nationwide educational seminars for executives (the role of her target job)
- Established relationships with in-house development executives in the Fortune 500 (who make purchase decisions about executive education)
- An MBA (credibility with and the ability to speak the language of the professors who staffed the executive education programs)
- Personal executive experience implementing changes and managing people (just like the target market for the executive education programs, establishing a link and credibility with program participants)

Diane got the job, has been promoted since, loves what she's doing now, and is certain she never would have gotten the chance without competitive advantages.

Sources and Examples of Competitive Advantages

Competitive advantages have many sources. Depth and breadth of knowledge, training, and work and life experiences are the most common. Competitive advantage statements can be used to show breadth if you have a strong technical background or to create focus if you have a generalist background. Experience in many areas of management information systems (MIS), such as application development, database administration, application architecture, and disaster recovery, is an example of breadth, as is an intellectual property lawyer's experience in trademarks, patents, and copyrights. Industry tenure is an example of depth.

Here are some other sources of competitive advantages, depending on your qualifications and job objectives:

- Unique industry or functional experience (or combination)
- Experience with an industry leader
- Knowledge of industry from multiple perspectives (e.g., worked your way up)
- Experience in a number of functional areas (such as advertising, marketing communications, market research, and branding for a marketing executive)
- Experience with different organizational stages (such as turnaround, start-up, maturity, or collapse)
- Experience with a particular situation, project, or issue (such as, downsizing, mergers and acquisitions, Six Sigma, total quality management, initial public offerings, bankruptcy)
- Unique and relevant training or education (e.g., an attorney with an MBA may be perceived to have an extra edge negotiating business deals)
- Experience with a target market, as a competitor or as a customer
- Experience with different kinds of companies, such as big and small companies, entrepreneurial and traditional, or domestic and international
- Ability to manage effectively through different organizational settings or situations

Why Competitive Advantages Work: The Story of Bill

The best way to show the power of competitive advantages is to contrast two different letters by the same candidate, one the standard letter that most of us write in response to an interesting position and the other a competitive advantage letter for the same job.

Here's the standard letter that my client Bill, a transportation executive, might have written using the approach to letters employed by most job seekers.

> Dear Mr./Ms. X:
>
> I am responding to your advertised position for a Regional Vice President with Company X that appeared in the June 23rd issue of the *Wall Street Journal*. As the enclosed resume indicates, I have more than 16 years of experience in the transportation industry, most recently at Company Y. I possess excellent management, operational, and sales skills.
>
> I look forward to meeting you.
>
> Sincerely yours,
>
> Bill X

This letter is a transmittal letter because all it does is transmit a resume to a prospective employer. It fails to market the candidate's unique qualifications for the job. As such, it's both a waste of an opportunity and a waste of paper. Contrast the impact of this letter with the sample competitive advantage letter Bill and I actually wrote. Each competitive advantage statement is italicized and numbered for easy reference.

> Dear Mr./Ms. X:
>
> I understand that Company X is seeking to fill the position of Regional Vice President. Having spent (1) *nearly two decades in transportation,* including being (2) *responsible for the development of Competitor Company Y's air and truck LTL freight service,* I am currently seeking an opportunity to lead a transportation organization, which is why your Regional Vice President position is so attractive to me. There are several additional reasons why I believe I am well qualified for such an opportunity:

- I am a "thinker and a doer" who has gained an accomplished (3) *understanding of the transportation industry through literally growing from a truck driver and dock man to president of a $100 million subsidiary of Competitor Company Y.*

- I have (4) *16 years of senior management responsibility with two of the transportation industry leaders.*

- During my tenure at these leading transportation companies, (5) *I created and managed Competitor Company Y's start-up forwarding company,* Company Y-1, and (6) *turned Competitor Company Z's special commodities division* into one of Company Z's few growing and profitable divisions.

In summary, these factors, along with my (7) *experience in the ocean, truck, air freight, rail and intermodal sectors,* makes me both interested in and appropriate for Company X's Regional Vice President position. I would be pleased to discuss the possible fit between your needs and my skills. Thank you very much for your time and consideration.

Yours truly,

Bill X

This letter builds a strong case beyond the resume. It draws direct factual links between the candidate's experience and the company's needs, using seven competitive advantages in the process. The letter accomplishes all these objectives in less than one page. By the way, Bill got the interview but turned down the job!

Chapter 17

Build a List of
Competitive Advantages

===

Secret: Your competitive advantages are your secret weapon.

===

Make the Right Career Move arms executives with the tools to beat the competition. Developed by the author, competitive advantages are a proprietary tool that has helped executives consistently prevail in job competitions. Competitive advantages are the secret, multiuse weapon to defeat the competition and land your dream job.

Your accomplishments define your brand by highlighting your distinctive contributions and results. No one is exactly the same kind of controller, trial lawyer, or chief executive officer. Defining your brand starts with accomplishments; the first way you distinguish yourself is through concrete results. Your resume presents the best, most representative array of those results.

Defining competitive advantages require stepping back from the details of these results for a macro view of your brand. Look at your accomplishments, experience, and skills to identify different themes about your distinctive areas of competence.

How? One CEO identified three major themes in her particular CEO brand: solving unsolvable problems (like commercializing products in record time and attracting top tier sales teams); being a change agent (from reinventing how sales reps are recruited and compensated to championing new approaches to the FDA drug approval process); and innovativeness in office infrastructure and training. These themes, and others she identified, were subsequently elaborated into a set of competitive advantage statements.

Once you've identified these different areas of distinctiveness, you can use them strategically to build your strongest case for an opportunity. The goal is to create a master list of competitive advantages from which you can build a customized case for a particular position or opportunity. That way, you're ready on short notice to put together a great resume cover letter, tailored to each opportunity.

Develop Your Master List

These five steps show you how to build your master list of competitive advantages:

1. *Begin by reviewing the accomplishments in your final resume and earlier drafts, as well as your performance reviews, lists of deals or projects, and so on.* Competitive advantages can incorporate information not on your resume because there is no place or need for it. Mine these sources for competitive advantage information.

   Step back from the details of accomplishments, experience, skills, and deals, and look for what is distinctive about your background and qualifications. What factual themes can you pull from specific achievements and experiences to *define your brand?*

2. *Use your accomplishments from all sources to identify objective, factual themes of success.* These qualifications may span several positions or accomplishments, whether they have to do with depth, breadth, or experience with a particular issue, challenge, growth stage, or group.

   The list of sources of competitive advantages in Chapter 16 is a starting point but should not limit the kinds of competitive advantages you identify.

3. *Look for objective examples in your list that you can use to demonstrate these themes.*

     For example: "Consistent record of managing multimillion-dollar system conversions to completion on time and on budget" or "75 percent of legal practice devoted to representation of early growth stage companies in the life sciences."

4. *List any significant awards or invitations to exclusive organizations based on your expertise and any unusual degrees that add to your particular qualifications.*

     For example, my clients have included a marketing executive with an engineering degree in a private utility, an information technology person with a JD who worked in a law firm, and a lawyer with an MBA who handled business transactions with the West in a third world country.

5. *Look for any training, talents, memberships, or other personal attributes or skills that are relevant to your list of qualifications.*

     I cite the example of a client competing for his dream job as head of a major environmental organization. He mentioned in passing that he had been a member of this international organization since the age of 10. We included this as one of the competitive advantages that helped him win the job, referring as it did to an objective indicator of lifelong interest in the organization and field.

Use the Competitive Advantages Worksheet to generate your master list of competitive advantages, using the listed categories as a starting point.

Write Competitive Advantage Statements

Maximize the impact of your competitive advantages by following these four simple guidelines:

1. *Write each competitive advantage statement as a separate bullet.*

     You can use them as separate bullets or incorporate them into sentences or paragraphs later on when you write your cover letters.

Competitive Advantages Worksheet

Use this worksheet to identify factual themes from your specific achievements and experiences. Accomplishments show what is distinctive about what you've achieved. Competitive advantages represent macro views of your brand: Use the following questions only as a starting point to help you define the themes.

Looking across your career, what is unique about your experience and skills? (Be factual.)

-
-
-

In what ways are your experience and skills broader than the competition's?

-
-
-

In what ways are your experience and skills deeper than the competition's?

-
-
-

Do you have unique industry or functional experience, or a combination?

-
-
-

Do you have unique or special and relevant skills and degrees?

-
-
-

Do you have experience with an industry leader?

-
-
-

(continued)

Competitive Advantages Worksheet *(Continued)*

Do you have experience with different organizational stages?

-
-
-

Do you have experience with a special and relevant situation, project, or issue?

-
-
-

Do you have experience with the target market as a customer or a competitor?

-
-
-

Do you have experience with different kinds of companies?

-
-
-

Have you won any awards or received special recognition?

-
-
-

Do you have special training, talents, or memberships?

-
-
-

What other themes distinguish your background?

-
-
-

2. *Make sure your statements are always factual and, whenever possible, quantitative.*

     Avoid subjective qualities or characteristics (e.g., "dedicated," "organized," "creative"). Forget vague or self-congratulatory assertions as well, such as "I have extensive experience in health care," "My strategic planning skills are excellent," or "Natural-born leader." This generic, undocumented fluff undermines your case. Leave out most if not all adjectives and adverbs.

3. *Trim the fat. Like accomplishments, competitive advantages gain power through brevity.* Several competitive advantages may be strung together in a paragraph in your letters, but individually they must be short and to the point.

     One great way to do this is to avoid spelling out implications. If your competitive advantages are relevant to an employer, you can safely assume that you don't need to belabor the obvious.

     For example, consider my transportation client's sample competitive advantage letter in Chapter 16. It wasn't necessary to point out that his experience growing up in the industry (competitive advantage #3)—as opposed to an MBA, who joins the industry in the management ranks—gave him a broader, more comprehensive, and operations-grounded understanding of the industry.

4. *Take the time to do it right. Like accomplishments, competitive advantages take work to define and polish.*

     A client once read me an ad and the letter he had written in response. He had several strong competitive advantages, but when the ad mentioned needing an energetic, hard-working multitasker, he wrote that he was "an experienced multitasker."

     I asked him how many projects he had ever handled at a time. He thought about it and figured it was 30. I pointed out that an objective statement like "Experience handling up to 30 simultaneous projects" was a far stronger competitive advantage. By putting in the effort to dig out a competitive advantage in factual terms, he made a much more impressive case for being an energetic multitasker. It had the added bonus of not pandering to the ad by just parroting the requirements.

Customizing Competitive Advantages for a Cover Letter

Now comes the fun part: putting your competitive advantages to work in a cover letter. In most circumstances, you'll include only three to seven competitive advantage statements. The goal is to convince, not overwhelm, your reader. Diagnosing a particular company's needs and telling a story with the competitive advantages you select is the best way to make an impact.

Diagnose Company Needs

This is a critical step. The unique combination of competitive advantages you present to an employer should create the greatest value for them and thus for your candidacy. This is how you turn competitive advantages into a real advantage. This section presents tips for identifying and selecting competitive advantages to build your case.

The unique combination of competitive advantages with which you tailor your case starts with diagnosing an employer's needs. Start with reading an ad's requirements, but ad or no ad, there is always more information to help you further customize your competitive advantages.

Investigate a company's current situation or prospects for information on priorities and problems to simultaneously clarify their needs and your potential value to them. Quick-and-dirty research is the objective—exhaustive fact finding is overkill. Contacts are a great source of inside information. Don't forget published and online sources, such as Business Index ASAP, www.bizjournals.com, and www.vault.com for up-to-date articles and information on a company and its executives. See Chapter 25 for additional assistance. Look for relevance and results as you diagnose needs and your demonstrated ability to meet those needs. Here are sample questions to ask as you read articles and talk to contacts about your target:

- *What are the latest developments in the company?* (Your competitive advantage question to yourself is: How can my particular skills and experience help the company benefit from these developments or minimize their negative impact?)

- *What are the major industry trends?* (Have I been up against the same trends in this industry or another? What have I learned or done that's relevant?)

- *Who are the company's primary competitors?* (Have I worked with, or competed successfully against, these competitors? If so, what specific experiences or achievements of mine can help this company?)

- *What is distinctive about the company's culture, reputation, products, or services, and so on?* (How is my background uniquely relevant? For example, do I have a great track record in marketing similar products? Do I have an Ivy League MBA and McKinsey experience, like most of the executive team? Do I have international experience that would be particularly helpful with the company's planned international expansion?)

- *What are the stated or unstated (from insiders) demands of the job?* (What about my background makes me the best person for the job?)

Careful diagnosis of employers' needs and the value you can create for them because of your unique combination of competitive advantages is the essential way to derive the full benefit from competitive advantages. Once you have customized your competitive advantages, you are ready to write a powerful cover letter.

Select and Revise Competitive Advantages from Your Master List: The Story of Kay

My client Kay was seeking a new opportunity with a law firm that provided more opportunities to work in the biotechnology field or in house with a biotechnology company. We developed the following master list of competitive advantages:

- Five years of experience managing multimillion-dollar cases (the content area of the cases to change depending on the target opportunity)
- Experience with one of the top 20 law firms in California, with an outstanding reputation in litigation
- Strong interest in science
- Extensive experience working with in-house counsel and senior management to implement programs to prevent future corporate risk and litigation, thereby averting potential liability for client companies
- Strong record of cost containment in managing litigation for Fortune 1,000 clients

Here's an example of the thinking process you'll go through to customize competitive advantages from your list to meet the needs of a particular employer.

I spent one evening helping Kay prepare a competitive advantage letter for her dream job in the general counsel's office of a prestigious biotechnology company. The daughter and wife of physicists, Kay had always had a strong interest in the sciences. She regretted having chosen not to pursue an undergraduate degree in science. She liked being a lawyer, but the chance to work at a biotechnology company and combine her interests in science and law seemed ideal.

At the outset, we started with a pretty weak case for this employer: Her list of competitive advantages included her interest in science and work for a prominent law firm, neither of which was much of a competitive advantage. The strikes against her were a lack of an advanced (even an undergraduate) degree in science, lack of in-house experience, particularly in biotech, and her career focus on insurance litigation.

Our challenge was to present her background in the strongest possible light, showcasing qualifications that made her an attractive candidate, despite some of her obvious deficiencies in terms of the standard job profile. We went through three drafts of competitive advantages en route to creating her most powerful list—and case.

In the evolution of competitive advantages that evening, I kept pressing for more specific information. I had her tally the percentage of her practice spent defending biotech (including pharmaceutical) and high-tech companies. The percentage turned out to be quite high: More than 90 percent of her clients were technology companies.

Pressed for something more compelling than an interest in science, Kay was able to enumerate her knowledge of complex scientific methods relevant to biotechnology, such as polymerase chain reaction and DNA amplification. This was a far cry in impact from a casual understanding or interest in science.

Still another competitive advantage was undergraduate coursework in biology, zoology, chemistry, organic chemistry, and physics—again, a far cry from a dilettante's interest in science. Do you know anyone besides a premed major who takes organic chemistry, much less for fun? This reinforced an enduring interest and background in science, a particular requirement of many biotechnology companies.

A final competitive advantage pointed to her high level of responsibility for major (multimillion-dollar) cases, including specific cases with biotech companies and with issues (such as trademark statutes) of interest to biotechs.

Wanting to make a powerful and succinct case, we used these changes and additions to the master list. We also chose to omit the competitive advantages about the top 20 firms and cost containment, as they were not as relevant to this opportunity.

Here's an excerpt from the final competitive advantage letter we prepared:

> Over 90 percent of my practice has been in the defense of pharmaceutical, biotech, and high-tech companies. During my tenure at Firm X, I have been responsible for managing cases involving complex factual and legal issues in both federal and state court. My qualifications include:
>
> - Substantive knowledge of complex scientific methodologies such as polymerase chain reaction, DNA amplification, and fractionation, in addition to immunology, oncology, and material science principles, gained during representation of biotech clients
>
> - Five years of experience managing multimillion-dollar cases, from the construction of a recent trademark statute for a small high-tech start-up to the application of new technology to proven legal doctrines for multinational pharmaceutical corporations, with an emphasis on quality work product while meeting budgets
>
> - Extensive experience working with in-house counsel and senior management to implement programs to prevent future corporate risk and litigation, each of which averted potential liability for client companies
>
> In addition, my enduring interest in the natural and physical sciences led me to take a variety of undergraduate courses in biology, zoology, chemistry, organic chemistry, and physics. My interest and knowledge of science, in combination with my legal experience, would enable me to make an important contribution to Company Y.

See Excerpts from Competitive Advantage Letters for other examples.

Excerpts from Competitive Advantage Letters

Here are additional examples of how competitive advantages can promote you in letters. Chapters 20 and 23 discuss how to use competitive advantages to promote yourself in interviews.

From a hospital executive seeking a job at the corporate headquarters of a major health care system:

During the past 11 years with leading hospitals in the XXX system, I have established a successful track record of designing, managing, and implementing major projects in food services, construction, and production. These projects have expanded and upgraded hospital programs, services, and facilities; consistently reduced costs; and increased revenues and patient satisfaction.

I have created many programs and systems to achieve substantial cost savings within the XXX system, from standardized menu and production systems at two hospitals, to merging elder care alliance hospital kitchens, to negotiating major vendor contracts that standardized product purchases at 40 hospitals.

From a lawyer and MBA seeking a job based in Russia handling business transactions with the West:

I function well in diverse cultural and business settings due to my broad experience and skills, including:

- An MBA and an extensive array of Silicon Valley business experience, including negotiation of a joint venture that is currently assembling and distributing personal computers in Russia
- Experience working closely with entrepreneurs in finding and structuring creative financing for the development, manufacture, and worldwide marketing of technologically sophisticated products
- Fluency in Russian

(continued)

From a Fortune 500 transportation executive looking for a CEO position with another Fortune 500 company in another industry:

First, I have a solid track record of performance for 20 years in a very challenging business, with 10 years of international experience, covering Asia, the Middle East, and Europe.

Second, there is great similarity between the XXX business and the XXX industry, namely, that both are asset intensive, highly networked, very competitive, difficult to differentiate product and service offerings, and require strong revenue management and dynamic intelligent pricing.

I have a record of successfully dealing with these challenges. For example, we have made extensive use of revenue management models at Company Y under my leadership, the result of which is improved margins and efficiencies in our network. We have also adopted the notion of dynamic pricing and have been successful in defining our products and offering differentiated pricing alternatives to our customers that have the simultaneous benefits of improved profitability and customer satisfaction.

Finally, as my career path shows, I have consistently been selected for or sought and handled significant challenges. These challenges have varied, whether they have to do with operations or tough markets, such as growing our market share in Los Angeles, or with people such as substantially upgrading our marketing team during my recent assignment in Tokyo.

Obviously, I could not do this alone. My ability to jump in and assume hands-on leadership for diverse responsibilities such as sales, marketing, operations, or reengineering and my ability to inspire others to perform at their best and to give them the coaching, resources, and tools to do their best have contributed to this success.

From a lawyer with experience in major law firms in New York and San Francisco, seeking a general counsel position with a high-end fashion retailer:

I am writing to inquire about the recently vacated General Counsel position at XXX. As the enclosed resume indicates, I have been practicing corporate law for nearly 10 years with two large international law firms in New York and California and have prior experience and training in the fashion industry.

More than 80 percent of my practice in New York was devoted to representing retail clients such as Prada, Barney's, and Steuben. During the two years prior to Company X's IPO, I functioned as its lead outside counsel, handling a broad array of responsibilities, from securitization financings to corporate restructurings. In addition, I am multilingual, studied fashion design at Parsons School of Design and the Fashion Institute of Technology, and worked at Ralph Lauren. I believe my background in fashion and law would suit Company Y's needs very well.

Chapter 18

Create a Competitive Advantage Story

Secret: Competitive advantages produce their
greatest impact in story form.

Whether you deliver your competitive advantages in written or oral form, you have about 30 to 60 seconds to capture your audience's attention. Done well, your competitive advantages create a unique picture of your qualifications that captivate a contact or prospective employer.

Competitive advantages assume their greatest importance when they tell a story. A collection of interesting facts is never as fascinating or persuasive as a well-told story that includes those facts. Your challenge is to tell the story—*your* story—in a memorable and relevant way to your audience.

A competitive advantage letter should be more than a laundry list of seemingly unrelated facts, even if presented in bullet points. What drives the selection of format—text, bullets, or a combination—is the story you have to tell and the best way to deliver it. The following questions can guide your choice.

The first question to ask is: What would this particular audience be most interested to learn about you? Your audience won't stay with you if they have to wait too long for something relevant, valuable, and unique. To deliver on relevance, value, and uniqueness, start strong. Isolate the most important competitive advantages for this audience and rank them in descending order of importance. This provides one kind of structure to the narrative you are constructing.

Second, are there themes across competitive advantages that add character and coherence to your story? For example, you might emphasize the theme of reinvention in your career because it is very much the situation of a prospective employer.

Finally, consider whether there are specific competitive advantages of unique significance to a particular employer that enhance your value and should be part of your story. Perhaps you sailed in the Americas Cup race and have firsthand knowledge of the boats a prospective employer makes. Or perhaps you successfully championed Six Sigma approaches to your corporation.

Tell a story, tell your story, stress its relevance, value, and uniqueness. Look for themes, order the points to the extent possible, look for larger themes to tie the competitive advantages together, spice things up with highly customized competitive advantages for this company or situation, and select a format that shows your story to best effect. That's the key to telling your best story.

The Power of a Competitive Advantage Story: The Story of Sarah

Sarah is a highly experienced administrator for a major professional services firm. Looking for a way to parlay her breadth of experience into a bigger general management role at a larger firm, we constructed a story that showcased her competitive advantages in a compelling narrative. Here is an excerpt:

> My experience with a major consulting firm for the past 18+ years typifies the changes professional service firms have experienced over the past two decades: Leading interdepartmental and interoffice task forces of up to 50 partners, associates, and staff, I have started up two new offices, managing subsequent rapid growth and downsizing. I have overseen six moves into new spaces and five build outs of existing spaces. These results, often

in short time frames and within stringent budgets, have all been accomplished on time and on budget.

I have been through mergers at the firm, office, and department levels. I have centralized financial systems and standardized operating systems from reception to time entry. I have managed our facilities in all areas, including budget, design and space planning, maintenance and security, ADA compliance, comfort, and cost-efficient ergonomics, consistently finding ways to standardize and streamline facilities operations and costs. While engaged in these activities at my full-time job, I managed to earn an MBA in Finance.

Sarah's competitive advantage story, further tailored to individual employers, provides her best case for a new job and a new role.

Career Tool 3: Interview Skills

Chapter 19

The Three Elements of Fit

===

Secret: You haven't done your interview job until you've demonstrated the three elements of fit.

===

Smart executives do dumb things in interviews. They talk too much about themselves. They focus only on what they want and what an employer can do for them. They volunteer negative information. They make claims that they don't bother to back up. They don't think beyond the surface meaning of questions, so they either answer the questions inappropriately or they lose opportunities to build their case. They confuse honesty with naivete. They concentrate on what they want to say and forget to listen. They let themselves become the victims of a poor interviewer who talks too much or asks poor questions. They don't ask thoughtful questions. They do not prepare compelling answers to common questions. In fact, they don't prepare or practice at all.

Interviews are the place to tell and sell your story. Interviews provide an opportunity to interact with a prospective employer, show who you are and see who they are, and investigate fit. It's a two-way street, after all. A successful interview requires more than simply showing up and spontaneously displaying your winning personality or track record.

The third element of market positioning is interview presentation. Coming into an interview with the other two elements in place—the resume and competitive advantages—puts an executive in an advantageous position. The resume positions you for the right job, and competitive advantages further position you for a particular job and employer. An interview brings these elements of marketing and positioning together in a face-to-face interaction that can close the deal.

Interview preparation takes positioning to the highest level: showing a prospective employer why you are the very best candidate for this opportunity. Done correctly, it demonstrates the three elements of fit:

1. Skills—Can you do the job?
2. Chemistry—Do you fit in the organization?
3. Motivation—Do you want the job?

The resume and competitive advantages address the skills and performance aspect of fit. The interview conclusively answers the skills question with detailed discussion of how an executive handled prior situations or would handle future situations. You must demonstrate convincingly that you have the skills and experience to excel at the job; otherwise, chemistry and motivation are irrelevant. Don't stint on this preparation.

Demonstrating chemistry and motivation is largely the province of the interview. Chemistry is there or it isn't—you can't and shouldn't try to manufacture it. But the valid assessment of chemistry requires a well-prepared interviewee so chemistry isn't obscured by the noise of poor preparation, unfocused answers, and poor questions. It requires that assessment of chemistry not be confounded with questions of performance or skill.

Chemistry also requires self-awareness. What are the most pronounced parts of your style? For example, how quickly do you make important decisions? How much time and information do you need to make these decisions? How do you react when forced to make decisions without the appropriate time and data? What are your hot buttons? What work environment, colleagues, organizational growth stage, or challenge motivate you? Demotivate you?

Chemistry requires awareness of others. What impact, positive and negative, do these aspects of style have on others? Awareness of your impact on others extends to the interview itself: Your ability to convey who you are as a person and an employee, as well as your ability to gauge prospective employers, depends in part on the ability to ask probing questions.

Motivation is another essential component of fit that can be measured only in interviews. This is the go-for-it piece. Do not make the potentially fatal mistake of assuming that hard to get is the only appropriate stance for a top executive. Don't let ego or pride lead you to confuse enthusiasm with desperation. If you want it, say so.

Remind an employer why you'll do a good job based on your past performance (e.g., "In my previous two positions, I repositioned struggling products and turned around underperforming business units. It's the kind of challenge I relish—and I'd especially enjoy the chance to help Company XXX regain market share").

An employer will hire the person who can do the job, will fit into the organization, wants to do the job, and will marshal enthusiasm as well as skill to do an excellent job. An employer is not planning to pay you big bucks for a half-hearted job. Your audition starts in the interview. Don't inadvertently skip a crucial part.

You haven't done your job until you've demonstrated skills, chemistry, and motivation in an interview. Demonstrate skills by linking your past performance to an employer's needs using competitive advantages and specific supporting incidents. Demonstrate chemistry by revealing your style and values, taking a stand that's important to you, and seeking points of contact. Demonstrate desire by letting an employer know you want the job. Don't expect others to take your fire in the belly on faith—show it.

Chapter 20

Before the Interview

Secret: You must *prepare* to be spontaneous.

The central paradox of a good interview is that its conversational and spontaneous tone can be achieved only through careful preparation and practice. There's no other way to ensure sounding spontaneous, conversational, and articulate rather than rambling and wordy. This chapter leads you through a step-by-step process to prepare for a winning interview.

Things to Do before the Interview

• *Research your target.* Interview preparation begins with researching the company and the position. A company web site and published materials are a useful place to start. Supplement web site information with published articles as well as inside information from your contacts.

Company materials, on web sites and in annual reports, are carefully and expensively designed to put the best face on a company's situation and prospects. In the case of annual reports, the information is not the most up to date. This information is important, but it is incomplete.

The Reference United States series of databases, available at many public and some university libraries, are Web-based subscription resources. Each database is subject specific, covering such areas as business and finance and health and medicine.

The Business Index ASAP database is particularly helpful. It includes several hundred magazines and newspapers, including all major business publications. It covers over 20 years of publications, with the most recent articles available in full text. The database is updated frequently.

Business Index ASAP lets you research companies, industries, executives, management issues, economic indicators, and business theories and practices worldwide. It provides instant access to business and academic journals with full text and images. You may search the database by company name or individual name, by business topic or keyword. Articles are displayed in reverse chronological order. If you want a hard copy, there is a printer-friendly version available or you can e-mail the article to yourself or others.

Why is this important? Business Index ASAP provides access to the latest published articles and those not produced by the company publicity machine. It gives you up-to-date information on a company, an executive, or an industry. A little current information helps you tailor your marketing messages and competitive advantages for the interview. Exhaustive research is unnecessary.

Inside information about the players, the politics, the history of the function or position, and the company is also useful. Your network can introduce you to insiders and provide you with relevant information.

This information, along with the information from Business Index ASAP and the company web site and publications, will help you tailor your marketing messages and anecdotes to the company, the position, and the interviewer, enabling you to make your best case to this company at this particular point in its history.

• *Define your marketing messages.* What messages do you want to deliver in the interview? One to three messages is generally ideal; more are likely to obscure your key points and wind up all over the map. An information technology executive interviewing for the first CIO position with a midsize company might list the following:

1. Ability to build and manage successful IT organizations from scratch
2. Ability to cut operating costs through automation
3. Ability to manage large system conversions on budget and on time

A litigator in private practice seeking a position in public service working for disadvantaged children could emphasize the following to demonstrate a lifelong commitment to and achievement in championing the rights of children:

1. Prior educational and professional experience in education, including a master's degree in early childhood education and work as a teacher and child care director in inner-city neighborhoods
2. Experience throughout her legal career doing pro bono cases and volunteer court advocacy on behalf of children
3. A strong record of successful client advocacy as a lawyer on behalf of corporate as well as pro bono clients

• *Identify relevant anecdotes and examples.* The next step is to identify specific stories or examples that support these marketing messages. Examples can elaborate on accomplishments in the resume or introduce new material not on the resume that references other achievements of significance to a particular interview audience. Examples can also enliven responses to common questions, such as "What is your management style?" and "What is the biggest failure you've experienced in your career?"

Specific stories lift answers out of the clichés such questions often demand. For example, the management style question almost begs for a clichéd response, such as "A participatory style" or "Management by walking around" or "Setting goals and letting others implement them on their own."

In contrast, the following response adds specificity and credibility: "Whenever we begin a project, I get the entire team together, and as a group we jointly decide on the timetable, deliverables, and assignments, then we have group meetings of the entire team to report on progress every two weeks."

Similarly, if your research has shown that a company is planning a major international expansion, prepare an anecdote about the time you were sent to establish your employer's first sales support organizations in Canada and Japan (on a week's notice, in the case of Canada) and grew the business dramatically within the first year.

• *Prepare answers to common questions.* Expect and prepare for common questions: why you are leaving your current position or employer, your greatest strength and greatest weakness, your greatest success and greatest failure. No one may ask these questions. But with preparation, you can volunteer this information to reinforce your marketing points.

Why are you leaving? You can prevent this question from being asked if in your response to "Tell me about yourself" or "What are you interested in?" you say how you are looking to build your career and contribution next. If you do get the question, remember to keep your answer positive, short, and poised: A longer than necessary response or the slightest trace of nervousness in your delivery will cause the interviewer to think you may be hiding something, such as having been fired.

A short answer, such as the following, says nothing negative about your employer or yourself and focuses on the future, all advantages in a well-crafted response to this potentially difficult question: "I'm a corporate attorney, and though my experience at Law Firm X has been great, it is primarily a litigation firm. I'm eager to be part of a firm that has a bigger corporate practice with more opportunities to do deals."

What's your greatest strength? Here it is useful to list several strengths briefly. The interviewer wants to hear a few things you believe you do well, not a long discourse on all the great things about you. For example, "Organizational skills, writing skills, and the ability to work well with people at all levels" has an appropriate level of detail and specificity.

What is your greatest weakness? The rule of thumb for this question is to list an actual weakness of yours that might seem a strength to a prospective employer, such as a propensity to drive yourself to meet a deadline, even if it means doing things for your staff instead of letting them do things for themselves. Even if you can't find a weakness of yours that meets this test, at least avoid using a weakness that doesn't even appear to be a weakness (e.g., "I care too much about my customers"—oh please!) or a weakness that could be fatal ("I'm a perfectionist and am never satisfied with the work product"—this might make an employer worry about missed deadlines unless you specifically mention you've never missed a deadline).

What is your greatest success or achievement? As this is a job interview, assume that the listener wants to hear about a work success. Pick a specific success or achievement (avoid general statements such as "My record of exceeding sales goals") in favor of a specific success, such as the time you exceeded the sales goal by 50 percent. As part of your answer make sure you tell how you achieved this success, not just what it was, and also what it is about you that was instrumental in achieving the success (such as the persistence to track down every elusive prospect).

What is your greatest failure? As a former search consultant and hiring manager, I urge you to prepare this answer carefully. There is nothing more irritating than someone who can't think of a failure or offers up something so vague or so lacking in individual responsibility that it hardly answers the question. Failing to answer this question with a genuine failure sends the inadvertent signal that you are a person who cannot accept responsibility for mistakes and thus cannot learn from them.

What makes for a good answer? Pick a legitimate but modest failure of yours, tell the listener about it and what you did wrong, and then make sure to tell what you learned from the experience. Everyone makes mistakes, but if you learned from them, you presumably won't repeat them.

Here's an example of a good answer to the failure question: "My first sales management job was a big one. I was managing a team of 10 sales reps and we were under such pressure to build revenues fast that I made assignments to experienced salespeople but didn't do the necessary follow-up. I just assumed that they could be counted on to make their quotas as I always had done and that they'd let me know if there was a problem. I found out the hard way that that isn't so, and that you always need to be following up with folks, especially when you are establishing relationships with them and don't know if they are comfortable bringing problems to you. I never make that assumption anymore. I learned that good delegation and good management require follow-up. We didn't make our quota the first quarter because of my mistake—but we exceeded it every quarter since."

Preparing answers to common questions such as these gives you good answers for the interview and good information to convey even if the questions aren't asked.

• *Define competitive advantages for the opportunity.* The most important question in any interview is the one that is rarely asked: Why hire you? Why are you the right person for this job? But if you leave any interview without providing a knock-their-socks-off answer to this unvoiced question, you have failed to achieve your most important objective in the interview.

Competitive advantages tailored to the particular opportunity are the way to create an unforgettable impact. This is why someone will hire you: because you can make the strongest factual and relevant case for your skills and experience in terms that matter to the employer. Your winning personality or your claims that you have "great skills and I know I can do the job for you" cannot and will not do the job. Earlier chapters helped you delineate your competitive advantages: Do not overlook this crucial part of your preparation.

• *Practice, practice, practice.* Like the old adage about the three most important factors in real estate—location, location, location—the most important factors in interviews are practice, practice, practice. Practice in front of a mirror, practice with a friend or family member, say answers out loud to yourself. Do not memorize answers—practice responding in different ways to the same questions. Get comfortable articulating your answers in a crisp and focused fashion. An interview coach and a video recorder can help.

Even if you make your living based on your presentation skills—for example, as a sales executive or a litigator—don't presume that an interview is the same kind of situation. You are selling yourself, not a company, a client, or a case. That makes the situation unique. No amount of charisma and charm is an adequate substitute for preparation and practice. Practice—practice—practice!

Chapter 21

The Importance of
Interview Questions

**Secret: Excellent questions are as important
as excellent answers.**

Don't miss out on major opportunities to stand out from the competition and gather useful information. Nailing an interview does not depend exclusively on having strong answers to an interviewer's questions. You tell a lot about yourself by the kinds of *questions* you ask. Thoughtful (versus off-the-cuff) questions are a great way to reveal your experience and perspective.

Similarly, you can tell a lot about an employer and an opportunity by asking thoughtful questions. Remember that an interview is a two-way opportunity to assess fit. To get the best information, avoid direct questions with "right answers" in favor of oblique questions that gather behavioral data so you can make your own evaluation of an issue or concern.

Preparing questions to ask an interviewer is as important as preparing answers to common questions. Follow these guidelines: Ask big picture questions; use questions to obtain information rather than to show off your knowledge; ask questions, then be quiet and listen to the answers; and ask indirect and objective questions to obtain useful and accurate information. These guidelines are elaborated next:

- *Ask smart questions to show what you know but not to show off.* You can tell a lot about yourself—your level of expertise, knowledge, sophistication, experience—by the questions you ask. A COO with 20 years of experience would ask different questions from a COO with 10 years of experience. Even the same COO would ask different questions at different points in his or her career. Experience breeds awareness of issues, obstacles, and concerns. Demonstrate your expertise by asking thoughtful and smart questions.

Don't pretend to ask a question and turn it into an opportunity to show how smart and knowledgeable you are. You know, the kind where a person ostensibly begins by asking a question, but it turns into an interminable lecture on what he or she knows. Nothing is more irritating to your audience. This is a smart-aleck question, not a smart question. And it is particularly easy to fall into this trap if you are the proverbial overachieving smart kid, as most executives are. Ask a thoughtful question and shut up.

During an interview practice with a smart client a couple of years ago, he asked interminable questions that showcased how much he knew about his prospective employer. When we debriefed later, I advised him to ask the question and stop talking. He insisted, "But I already know that information."

I replied, "Would it be so terrible if the interviewer told you something you already knew?" Used to being the guy who knew all the answers, he was shocked by my response, but it made him realize he was undermining his own effectiveness by showing how much he already knew.

What's an example of a smart question? A smart question may be as varied as one about the impact of Sarbanes-Oxley on the human resources department, the company's major challenges in the China market, the perceived impact of law firm mergers on local boutique firms like the one you are talking to, a technical point of business in the industry, or a recent development in the industry or with a major competitor. There are all kinds of smart questions, but what matters most is that as a critical part of your investigation you think carefully about what you would like to know about prospective employers, their business, and how they approach it.

- *Ask strategic questions.* Your questions tell a lot about you in another way: Asking strategic, big picture questions reinforces your self-presentation as an executive. An executive who focuses primarily on tactical and micro issues (e.g., What are the major responsibilities of this position?) without first investigating their strategic context (e.g., the major challenges facing the company, its primary competitors, how this position will help the company confront its primary challenges) contradicts the image of you as a player.

And forget questions about benefits, compensation, and vacations. Nothing is more certain to raise red flags for your audience. Job offers won't be extended or accepted without a discussion of compensation and benefits, so don't risk suggesting that you are interested primarily in these things instead of the work challenges and opportunities.

- *Ask bold questions.* Remembering the dual importance of demonstrating qualities and gathering useful information in an interview, consider asking bold questions to serve both purposes. A question such as "Is there any way in which I don't meet your ideal profile for this job?" or "Do you have any reservations about my candidacy?" gives you the advantage of the startle effect. It takes a lot of confidence to ask a bold question like this, a good quality to convey to a prospective employer.

More important, interviewers are generally so surprised by this unexpected question that they are apt to answer candidly. This provides you with useful information about unexpressed concerns, information an interviewer is unlikely to share otherwise. Armed with this information, you now have a perfect opportunity to overcome the hidden objections.

- *Ask oblique questions to gather useful information.* Your questions also serve another purpose: to gather critical information on fit. Here especially I recommend what I call "oblique" questions to gather objective data.

Too often, executives ask questions with obvious right or wrong answers. "Is this a team environment?" is a particularly common one. A team environment is so socially desirable that it is the rare interviewer who would respond "No." This may be because he or she doesn't wish to portray the company in an unflattering light, particularly to a desirable prospective employee. Or the interviewer may genuinely, and dementedly, believe it is a team environment.

In the latter case, you are depending on the subjective evaluation of a person you don't know. In fact, this person might not know a team environment if it bit him or her on the leg (as team environments are wont to do), due to blind spots or utter cluelessness.

For all these reasons, you can generally obtain better, more objective information by asking straightforward, behavioral questions with no obvious right or wrong answers. This approach lets you evaluate the data and draw your own conclusions about things like the team environment.

Questions satisfy these requirements more readily if they assess an issue in a nonobvious or oblique fashion. In the case of team environment, oblique questions such as the following can provide better information for reaching your own conclusion about whether it's a team environment or the kind of team environment in which you would feel comfortable:

- How often does the group meet?
- What does the group discuss at these meetings?
- Tell me about the last time the group faced a crisis. What happened? How was it resolved? Who was involved in reaching this resolution?
- Who makes decisions on project or case assignments?
- Tell me about major projects the group is handling. Who is involved?
- How frequently do people work on projects together or handle projects alone?

Asking several questions provides you with objective data to make your own assessment of the team environment, or any other element of the position or company you want to investigate.

In sum, by devoting as much attention to preparing your questions as preparing your answers, you make the most and the best of any interview.

Chapter 22

During the Interview

**Secret: Focus the interview on filling a
business need, not a personal need.**

The purpose of an interview is to determine if you can meet an employer's business need. Your personal need for career fulfillment or happiness is secondary to the employer's and important only if you meet the business need.

Too many people lose sight of this. It reminds me of a client in the final interviews for a potentially dream job. He was telling me how the employer would have to do this, have to meet this criterion, needed to convince him about their strategic plan. I interrupted him to say, "Jack, that's their job. Your job is to convince them that they want you. Why don't you focus on your job and let them focus on theirs?"

It is easy to get caught up in an interview and lose this focus, particularly when asked common questions such as "What do you want to do?" or "Why are you interested in this job or company?" Too often the response to these questions is something like "I want a job with a market leader with lots of challenges and opportunities for advancement, where I can be part of the management team setting the strategic direction for the company." The result is often an answer that sounds like "me me me." By keeping your eye on the business need to be filled, you can provide a more compelling response.

The analogy I use is that of a kaleidoscope: If you turn it the slightest bit in one direction, the pieces fall into a certain pattern; with a slight adjustment, the pieces form a wholly new pattern. Similarly, if your response to questions like this is "I do these things very well and this job provides an opportunity to do those things," the difference in spin creates an enormous difference in impact.

Here is an example of an answer that demonstrates a good way to highlight what you do well, as well as why you want to do it: "Throughout my career, I have been particularly successful in entrepreneurial companies that need someone to build IT departments and teams with limited resources and time. This is what I love to do and do best. Company X represents an opportunity to do this for a company that is changing the multimedia software industry."

• *Demonstrate value (quantify your impact)*. When looking to make a positive impression on a prospective employer, the most effective strategy is to show the difference you have made by using specific and relevant examples that quantify the impact of your actions or contributions.

One of the most common interview mistakes is to declare or claim skills or expertise rather than presenting facts that showcase skills or expertise. A star litigator client made this mistake with such statements as "I have excellent presentation skills" and "I can handle big cases" instead of concentrating on more factual claims such as "I second-chaired a million-dollar case that saved a Fortune 500 manufacturer over $10 million."

• *Listen carefully*. Your marketing messages, examples and anecdotes, and competitive advantages are important parts of your self-presentation. Do not get so focused on what you have to say that you forget to listen carefully to the interviewer's questions and comments. It is an easy mistake to make in the highly charged atmosphere of an important interview.

I worked with a senior executive, Jessica, a smart and competent real estate executive. As I coached her for an important interview, I remarked that her answers were good, but they did not answer my questions. She was not listening. She seemed scripted, determined to convey messages, and not interested in what I was asking. I repeatedly hammered home this message through several interview sessions.

Here's what happened to Jessica. In the initial interview for the dream job she eventually won, two executives used a list of prepared questions to interview her. After asking several questions from the list, they quietly put the list face down and began a less structured conversation with her. Later, after several subsequent interviews, when they offered the job to her, they mentioned, "We were very impressed by how carefully you listened."

Although this was a particularly dramatic example of the importance of listening, it is important for everyone in every interview.

• *Demonstrate qualities.* Jessica's thoughtful listening to a prospective employer's questions and concerns, as well as her thoughtful responses to what she heard, were instrumental in her hiring.

An interview is an opportunity to demonstrate qualities. If you are marketing yourself as a strategic thinker, you must be prepared to give strategic, big picture answers, instead of focusing primarily on tactical issues.

I remember an interview coaching session with a partner at a major law firm. When asked in the practice interview for his greatest strengths, he mentioned his highly organized approach. When we debriefed his answers afterward, I noted, "If you are so highly organized, why were your answers so rambling and disorganized?"

I was not trying to be flippant or mean. I was simply observing how his answers came across. Prospective employers may not be as critical of interview responses as I am paid to be, yet interview responses that are at odds with how you are marketing yourself are bound to undermine your candidacy. Get clear on what qualities you want to demonstrate and make sure you demonstrate them.

• *Volunteer information to make your points.* Sometimes the information you volunteer in an interview is as important as, or more important than, how you respond to questions you are asked.

Let me share an example. As a search consultant, I helped an environmental consulting firm hire a critical #2 person for its fastest growing office. Business development was a critical requirement for the successful candidate. The candidate who was eventually hired was the only candidate who, before we even got to questions about business development, spoke like an entrepreneur. In talking about current clients, she said things like "I know I can bring this client with me" and "I am convinced we can get a lot of hazardous waste work from this organization."

Her spontaneous offers of information on business development made a more persuasive case than anything she could have said in response to questions about business development. Although it was not the only reason she was hired, it was certainly a significant factor. And its impact was strengthened by the fact that she volunteered this information without having to be asked for it.

There is another important reason why it pays to be prepared for an interview. Bad interviewers are the rule rather than the exception. Their most common failing is to talk too much—and secondarily, to ask poor questions. Without preparation, it is easy to leave an interview feeling that you have failed to make your best case.

By being prepared, you can conversationally and casually make your points. Interjecting comments such as "That reminds me of when we restructured our international subsidiary" is a subtle way to wrest control of the conversation. You can take this opportunity to mention relevant anecdotes, marketing messages, or competitive advantages. At the same time, you impress an interviewer by spontaneously offering up useful information without having to be asked.

- *Don't confuse honesty and naivete.* The best example of confusing honesty and naivete was the time I asked one executive, "What is your greatest weakness?" He replied, "Poor judgment." I thought the comment showed such poor judgment that I had to restrain myself from leaping across the conference table and shaking him by the lapels. Luckily, it was a practice interview!

Too often, in a principled (and misguided) desire to tell the truth, the whole truth, candidates like this one end up looking foolish. In interviews, as in life, being honest does not mean divulging confidences, spilling your guts, or volunteering serious weaknesses.

This applies to a broad range of common questions, from your greatest weakness or failure to your worst boss, what you like best and least about your current job, and even where you see yourself in five years. The point is not to say whatever a prospective employer wants to hear. You cheat yourself as well as an employer if you choose to say the ingratiating thing, not the truth. But it's also important to be thoughtful in your responses.

Telling an employer that in five years you want to be running your own company is not likely to make them interested in investing in you; saying that you dislike the bureaucracy and politics in your current position is unlikely to endear you to a bigger company with a reputation for turf wars, but it should make you consider your targets more carefully.

In the film *Broadcast News*, the character played by Albert Brooks says, "Wouldn't it be great if neediness were a turn on?" It got a lot of laughs. Neediness isn't attractive. Nor are other serious frailties. Don't count on a prospective employer being charmed and disarmed by the unvarnished—and wildly unflattering—truth. They are more likely to be alarmed.

Following these guidelines will help you make the most of an interview, keeping your eye on the ball—filling a business need, not a personal need—and making your best case to do so.

Chapter 23

The Top Interview Requirement

Secret: Always answer the one question that is rarely asked.

Remember that telling a prospective employer why you are the best person for the job and why they should hire you is your top priority in the interview. Don't prepare your competitive advantages for the job and then forget to mention them in the interview. This is easy to do as it's unlikely you will get a direct question about why you are the best person for the job.

You may wonder how to introduce competitive advantages if no one asks for them. Simple: Because you are well prepared, you can conversationally insert a statement near the end of the interview, such as, "Well, Bill, I am very enthusiastic about this opportunity and I believe I'm the right person for this job. Let me tell you why: I have 12 years of experience working for your top competitors and I've been consistently rated as one of their top salespeople in the United States. I have a master's in electrical engineering, so I understand the technical specifications better than most salespeople and can talk to buyers with a lot of credibility. And finally, I have had three successful experiences building sales organizations from scratch in record time, much like the one you are planning to build."

Your number one responsibility in an interview is to provide a compelling answer to the "Why hire you?" question before the interview is over. The fact that this question is almost never asked doesn't diminish the importance of your providing an answer. Don't leave an interview without answering it. Use the blank Why Hire You Worksheet at the back of the book to prepare your response for each interview.

Why Hire You Worksheet

Important facts about the company:

-
-
-

My relevant career/job history:

-
-
-

My relevant accomplishments:

-
-
-

My competitive advantages:

-
-
-

Relevant anecdotes or examples to support competitive advantages:

-
-
-

Questions to ask:

-
-
-

Chapter 24

After the Interview

**Secret: The interview isn't over when
you shake hands and say good-bye.**

Doing the necessary follow-up after the interview will ensure that you make and learn the most from an interview. Noting problems with the interviews and remembering to thank those who interviewed you are the two most important forms of follow-up:

- *Record problem questions and answers.* Immediately after the interview, record any questions that caused you problems and answers with which you were not completely satisfied. This is where your future preparation efforts need to focus extra attention. It is important to record this information right away, as you are apt to forget it once the adrenaline rush of the interview subsides.

- *Send thank you notes.* Aside from the common courtesy of thanking people for spending time with you, a common courtesy unfortunately infrequently practiced (that alone has made many candidates stand out), thank you notes provide an opportunity to make an important point you overlooked in the interview or to reinforce or draw together points you did make. It is also a place to respond on further reflection to comments or questions of the interviewer, and as such, a chance to show you were listening. Do not overlook this important step.

Here's an example of a brief yet effective thank you sent by a corporate attorney seeking a position with a blue-chip Silicon Valley boutique law firm:

Thanks so much for the opportunity to meet the entire Corporate team and to learn about your exciting work with life sciences companies. Having spent a couple of years at the FDA early on in my career, I am confident that my regulatory experience and contacts could help the firm and its clients through the approval process and bring great medical devices and drugs to consumers sooner.

In addition, my experience on some of the major Valley deals in the life sciences sector during the past five years has given me the opportunity to work with the major players and learn the best practices for closing complex deals successfully and on a timely basis. It was interesting that Tom and I had similar ideas about how to streamline the deal process and I'd enjoy the chance to discuss the templates idea in more detail. I would welcome the chance to be part of Life Sciences Law Group.

FINDING THE RIGHT JOB

Chapter 25

Job Search Strategies to Optimize Time and Impact

**Secret: A successful job search depends more on
how you do it than on what you do.**

Virtually all my clients are dissatisfied and frustrated by prior attempts to find more satisfying work. These successful people have been singularly unsuccessful in their job-seeking efforts. Why? Most executives know the basic ways to find a job. What they don't know is how to use these strategies effectively. This is the difference between success and failure.

I remember the executive who, at our first meeting, described his prior job search efforts: letters sent to more than 200 search firms and more than 300 employers, informational interviews with more than 150 people, 10 versions of his resume, responses to more than 100 ads. But no job. No wonder he was discouraged. He had come to the same erroneous conclusion that many of my clients reach, namely, that he wasn't employable.

What I wanted to tell him was that he had conducted 145 unnecessary informational interviews, sent 500 worthless broadcast letters to search firms and companies, produced nine superfluous resumes, and wasted time responding to most of the 100 ads. I restrained myself, saying only that he should stop his job-seeking activities until we had had a chance to clarify his targets, work on his resume and other job search tools, and reevaluate job search strategies. Please follow the *same* advice until after reading this chapter, which outlines the strategies, tactics, and game plan to optimize your job search.

Most executives know the traditional strategies for finding a job: network and personal contacts, ads, search firms, and research and direct contact with employers. A fifth strategy, online networking, is a less well known but important variation on the networking strategy and a useful addition to your job search efforts. People get jobs using all five strategies, so it is important to use all of them. However, because the contacts strategy has a yield rate greater than the other four combined (70 percent to 80 percent of all jobs, by most estimates), this strategy deserves proportionately greater emphasis.

The lines among the strategies are blurred, because you can and should use contacts with each strategy (e.g., even if you hear of an opportunity through an ad, use your network to get to people within the company to gather more information and, if you are lucky, to get introductions to decision makers or those with influence on the hiring decision).

Similarly, leverage information resources and research with all job search strategies to increase their effectiveness. This chapter contains suggestions about information resources and strategies. Turn to Appendix E for a thorough discussion of the importance of research and information to a successful job search and recommended information resources.

Strategy 1: Networking

Networking may be a cliché, but developing and maintaining a strong network is crucial. Developing and maintaining your network while you still have a job and presumably don't need one is a wise investment of time and energy. It requires more than a signature at the bottom of an annual holiday card. Spending time to get to know people and to help them when they need assistance is essential to developing a network that you can count on. This includes search consultants.

Go out of your way when others ask for your help, providing contacts, introductions, search leads, and the like. They won't forget, and it will make it much easier and more productive to pick up the phone and ask for help in return. And don't forget to return calls from unemployed contacts; unreturned calls are the biggest gripe and blow to the morale of job seekers. Remember to make time for people so they make time for you. It's basic (but unfortunately uncommon) human courtesy, and people will remember it.

One of the most frequent resolutions my clients make is to keep up their networks. It is a challenge in light of the demands of executive schedules. But if you schedule a couple of lunches a month, or use your PDA or your administrative assistant to remind or schedule you, you can make it happen.

Four Steps in Working Your Network

1. *Generate a master list of contacts.* Brainstorm to create a comprehensive list of useful contacts, not just people who could hire you. You never know where the crucial contact will come from; frequently it comes from an unlikely place, such as a casual acquaintance or a telephone conversation with a former colleague of your neighbor.

Check your address book, holiday card lists, social and business files, as well as directories. Remember friends, relatives, professional and alumni associations, clubs, sororities or fraternities, former housemates, past employers, friends who have changed jobs, and service providers such as lawyers and dentists. These direct contacts will refer you to an indirect list of contacts, people who form a bridge between you and the decision makers in target companies.

2. *Cast a wide net when putting together your list of contacts.* A very common mistake is to generate too small a list of contacts, generally limited to individuals in your profession and location. This is wrong! You know people in other professions and locations, and so do your contacts. Your goal is to cast as broad a net as possible, and then to expand it further by getting at least one contact from each of your contacts. This first step alone will double the size of your network.

3. *Categorize contacts by the type of assistance desired, as your approach to them will vary accordingly.* For example, can an individual provide information about a company or industry? Names of other contacts in the target industry or companies? Can the individual hire you? Refer you to decision makers or people who can hire you? Provide introductions? Provide information on an industry and how to approach decision makers in that industry? Give you advice on your job search campaign? Raise awareness of your availability?

4. *Give thought to the order of your approach.* Do not yield to the temptation to contact the heavy hitters first. Although it is true that they may be able to hire you and thus bring your job search to a rapid close, the fact is that you are likely to get only a single pass at these people. To make your best impression, you want to be well practiced and polished, which will take some time. It is better to start with a less demanding audience, gain practice and confidence in presenting yourself, and then contact the heavy hitters.

Tips for Working Your Network

• *Ask for something specific.* Among the many mistakes I have personally made with contacts is the vague request. Born of discomfort with asking people for things, I would call someone and announce, "Jack, listen. I've decided to leave Company X," leaving the sentence unfinished, hoping that Jack would interrupt to say, "Shelley, I know of the perfect thing for you."

Jack—and Jill—never did know of the perfect thing, of course. So I would go on, after a pause, to add, "So if you hear of anything that uses my organizational, communication, and interpersonal skills, please let me know." That didn't work much better. It certainly won't work when you are trying to change directions, as your network is apt to think of you in terms of your prior position—the very thing you may be looking to change.

Avoid vague requests like "If you hear of anything, let me know" or "I've decided to leave and I wondered if you had heard of any openings." This is another example of overburdening your audience. Instead, be direct, succinct, and specific: "Could you introduce me to your clients in biotech companies?" is better than "Do you know anyone who might have an opening?"

A request like the following is much more likely to get results: "I know you consult to the biotechnology industry. Do you have any clients [perhaps list specific target company names] I might talk to about opportunities?"

Lest you fear that a specific request may limit the help contacts may provide, remember that your role is to facilitate their assistance, not to overburden them with open-ended requests that appear as though you are asking them to figure out what you should do or where you belong. Contacts can always volunteer additional ideas—just make sure that you frame your requests specifically so they have a good idea of how to help.

- *Get to the point quickly.* To make your contacts more effective, remember to let others know ASAP the reason for your call or letter. We have all been on the receiving end of contacts from long-lost colleagues who call out of the blue and schmooze seemingly endlessly until they get down to the real reason for the call. This just irritates the very people whose help you are trying to enlist.

To avoid this problem, after some brief small talk, come to the point quickly about the reason for your call. Do the same thing with your letters. When I was in executive search, I would say, "I know you are busy, so let me get straight to the point of my call." This strategy produced a consistently positive reaction.

- *Help others help you.* Make it easy to help you. You can do this in several ways. First, say what you're seeking (specify your target). Next, summarize your qualifications. Finally, state what you want from your contact.

Being focused, succinct, and explicit will generate a much better response from your network. When appropriate, let your contacts know they can use the information in your letter as a script in making calls on your behalf.

- *Always make the next step yours.* Never ask someone else, even a dear friend, to let you know if he or she thinks of a person or opportunity to pursue. And don't agree to someone's offer to call you back after he or she has checked around. Your job search is your number one priority and no one else's; make sure you put the onus *explicitly* on yourself to follow up. Tell them, "I'll give you a call back. Would a week give you enough time to contact your clients or partners?"

• *Look for ways to reciprocate.* Networks are powerful when they are two-way relationships. What makes it hard to network is the one-sidedness of the request. But if you offer information and assistance to others—candidates and sources to search consultants, up-to-date market information to colleagues—you reinforce relationships as well as make it easier to make contacts. Get in the habit of asking, "What can I do for you?"

The Initial Contact

What's the best way to reach your contacts? The question is not "By letter or by phone?" but rather "Which one first?"

• *Contact everyone by phone and by letter.* Consider such factors as the recency of your previous contact, the nature of your relationship, the person's travel and business schedule, which approach is your strength, but do use both strategies with everyone. This will provide each contact with the best and most complete information and will increase the chances of a face-to-face meeting, which is the best source of introductions, referrals, and information.

As a later section describes in more detail, e-mail is generally preferable to snail mail as a way to send a letter to an executive. E-mail will reach an executive on the road, is available to check 24/7, and is less likely to be screened and weeded out by assistants or secretaries. Send your cover letter and resume as attachments rather than in the text of the e-mail to preserve formatting.

• *Research first before contacting:*
   —Do library and online research prior to contacts with personal network, target companies, advertised positions.
   —Obtain published company materials and/or check out the company's web site.
   —Most important, look for recently published information from outside sources (e.g., Business Index ASAP, Reference

United States, your local business journal, www.bizjournals .com). See Appendix E for additional information.

When to Start with a Letter

- To break the ice after a long hiatus
- When your contact travels a lot
- When there's an impenetrable wall of voicemail and/or secretaries
- When you are better at writing letters than speaking on the phone

E-mailing is acceptable, and more and more seems to be the most practical way to reach busy and traveling contacts.

Writing has two advantages over calling: It breaks the ice, and it eliminates the awkward telephone schmooze fest that ensues when you call someone out of the blue.

When to Start with a Call

- When you know your contact well and he or she would be put off by the formality of an initial approach by letter
- When time is short
- When you are better at speaking on the phone than writing a letter

Following Up the Initial Contact

Following Up a Letter

- Follow up with a phone call within the time indicated in your initial letter (two weeks or less).
- Don't leave more than one message.
- Call back at odd times (early, late, lunchtime) to catch your contact, not an assistant.
- Make friends with the assistant (find out good times to call, be polite, let the assistant know you prefer to make the calls rather than leave messages).

Following Up a Call

- Follow up the phone conversation with a letter with all the specifics (your target, qualifications, what you want from the contact).
- Do this even and especially with close friends who would be embarrassed to ask what you do or are looking for.
- Encourage people to borrow from your letter when making calls or introductions on your behalf.

Tips for Networking and Contacts

- Don't immediately take "no meeting" or "no contacts" for an answer.
- The most effective job search strategy is the one people avoid most: networking.
- Don't be a dilettante: Devote plenty of time to networking so you get comfortable with it (the "wading-in-the-pool" phenomenon).
- Drop the "beggar" mind-set.
- Track the amount of time you spend on networking each day.

See the Sample Networking Letter and the Sample Telephone Script for examples.

Strategy 2: Search Firms

Another common mistake is too much reliance on search firms to uncover the right opportunity for you. That is not their role. Search consultants work for employers who have executive vacancies to fill; they do not work for you. Their focus is on finding the best person for a client. They are more likely to be interested in you if you happen to be right for one of their current assignments.

There are two kinds of search firms. Contingency firms are paid only if they make a placement. Retainer firms are paid regardless of whether they make a placement. In the case of the former, more

Sample Networking Letter

Ed Smith
EVP Operations
Pepsico
700 Anderson Hill Road
Purchase, NY 10577-1444

Dear Ed:

It's been quite some time since we last spoke. Hope the intervening years have been good ones for you, personally and professionally.

I've spent the past four years since I left Pepsi in a series of challenging operating roles, initially turning around the biggest division of Company X as General Manager, then moving on to COO of the entire company and doubling revenues in under three years.

It's been a busy and incredibly exciting time, but with the pending acquisition by Company Y, with its own strong executive team, the future opportunities look much more limited. So I've decided to start looking around for COO or President roles at Fortune 1,000 consumer products companies.

Which brings me to the reason for this letter, Ed. I know your contacts in the consumer products industry are extensive and that your personal endorsement counts for a lot. I was hoping that you would be willing to make some introductions for me at consumer products companies. Company Z and Company ZZ are companies that I believe are the size and growth stage for someone like me, but I welcome your counsel on appropriate targets as well as your introductions.

My background includes operating experience in Fortune 500 and 1,000 companies, turnaround experience, experience growing market share in a mature industry, and entrepreneurial

(continued)

experience building market share from scratch. I've managed all operating functions, from finance to logistics, and managed profitable P&Ls in almost every quarter for the past 15 years in a total of four companies. A resume is attached to give you an up-to-date view of my experience and skills.

I will plan to give you a call to follow up within the next two weeks, Ed. Thanks for your consideration. And please give some thought to what I can do for you in return.

Best regards,

Beth Williams

than one firm often handles the same search, as the company pays only the firm that presents the successful candidate.

The different fee arrangements largely dictate the methods used to identify candidates. Because their fee is not guaranteed, contingency recruiters typically present potential candidates who identify themselves to recruiters through ad responses or direct contact. By contrast, because only one retained firm is hired for a search and its fee is guaranteed, retainer firms typically do research and outreach to identify the most promising candidates for their searches. Retained firms generally handle higher level nonlegal executive searches.

In the legal field, the situation is not as clear-cut. Traditionally, legal searches have been handled on a contingency basis. Today, the situation is more variable. Almost all associate or junior-level searches are still filled on a contingency basis. Most partner searches are also contingency, but law firms are increasingly turning to retained searches to fill key hiring needs. In-house and firm-opening searches are more likely to be conducted on a retained basis.

There is another reason lawyers should not rely exclusively on search consultants: the long-standing industry focus on pedigree.

Sample Telephone Script

This is a sample conversation with a networking contact, Tom Jones.

Tom: Hello, this is Tom Jones.

You: Tom, this is Nancy Lawson. Jack Smith, a long-time colleague of mine at Company X, encouraged me to contact you. Is this a convenient time for you to speak?

Tom: Sure. How is Jack?

You: He has his hands full these days, managing the merger of Company X with Company Y. Which in fact is the reason for my call. I'm the CFO at Company X, where I have spent the past 12 years building the finance function from the ground up. We've doubled the size of the company domestically, expanded into Asia, led three acquisitions, and took the company public, all while remaining highly profitable.

But with this pending merger, we're approaching the size that means my job will be more about duplicating the same successes and maintaining performance. I'm an entrepreneur at heart and looking for an opportunity to build a financial function from scratch again. Jack said you are the person to contact because of your extensive contacts in the venture and high-tech communities.

Tom: Well, I have been an entrepreneur for a long time . . .

You: I was hoping we could arrange a meeting at a good time for you.

Tom: My schedule is pretty crowded.

You: I expected that. How about an early breakfast meeting?

Tom: I could probably fit that in.

You: How about next Friday at Buck's at 7:00 A.M.? Does that work for you?

(continued)

Tom: Sure.

You: In the meantime, Tom, why don't I shoot you a copy of my resume by e-mail so you get a better sense of my track record and which of your contacts might be worthwhile introductions for me. What's your e-mail address?

Tom: tom.jones@CompanyZ.com.

You: Great. I'll e-mail it to you today and call you Thursday to confirm. I look forward to meeting you, Tom.

As a general rule, legal employers, especially law firms, put primary emphasis on educational and professional credentials in hiring decisions throughout a lawyer's career, not just straight out of law school. Impeccable credentials—often coming from a top 20 or top 50 law school, serving on the *Law Review*, and working for an AmLaw 200 or 100 firm or a highly regarded smaller firm—are part of the desired pedigree. Legal search firms are often hired to find lawyers with this pedigree.

The result? If you are a highly degreed partner with a big book of business, especially in a hot practice area, or an associate with great credentials, legal search firms will be happy to represent you. With a less than stellar pedigree or book of business, search firms are less able to be of assistance. Of course, there are plenty of exceptions: Candidates with the right level of experience, the specific skill sets required by the client, and the interpersonal skills to achieve the client's goals are those who stand the best chance of being selected.

Regardless of the type of search consultant, the responsibility for finding the best fit for you remains squarely in your corner. Even contingency search consultants who may be motivated to market a person they think is a hot commodity and thus a likely source of a placement fee are still focused above all on pleasing their clients and getting their fees, rather than on whether a job is the best fit for you. You should not delegate this important role to anyone else.

This is not to take anything away from good search consultants who care deeply about candidate-job fit. However, you have the responsibility for managing your career, including making the best career choices for yourself. No one has the same investment you do in finding the right job for you, the one that in immediate and long-range terms meets your career goals best.

Another consideration that affects your use of search firms is cost. Search firms typically charge hefty fees to fill searches, 30 percent of annual compensation or more. This means that you come with a higher price tag if you are introduced by a search firm, which can make you a less attractive candidate. Some companies retain search firms to help them screen as well as recruit applicants—and your unsolicited resume may simply be referred to a search firm—but in many cases, a direct approach to an employer, especially if it comes through personal contacts, can get you further.

In some cases, a search firm can also be the only vehicle to get you in front of a particular company. However, just blanketing search firms with letters is an unproductive use of time and stamps (or e-mail). Having worked at one of the world's largest executive search firms, I can attest that they receive tens of thousands of unsolicited resumes a year. It is easy to get lost in the shuffle. And retained search firms pride themselves on finding their own top candidates through research and outreach, rather than relying on ads or unsolicited resumes.

On the other hand, if you can get a personal introduction to a particular search consultant from one of their current or former clients or candidates, you stand a much better chance of meeting with that person and getting special attention. Good search people are wonderful people to know and are important relationships to build.

Whether they have an appropriate opportunity or not, good search consultants can be an invaluable source of market information on topics from the general state of the market, to companies to pursue or avoid, the going rate for someone with your experience and skills, obstacles or challenges you will face in the market, and advice on how to overcome these obstacles or challenges.

As with any relationship in your network, the key is reciprocity and longevity. Too often, job seekers are focused on what a recruiter can do for them, instead of actively looking for what they can do for a recruiter. Look for ways you can help, such as by providing names of possible candidates or sources for their available searches and offering to provide information on a company or industry or possible candidates. Whether a search consultant has an appropriate opportunity or not, your goal is to build a long-term relationship. And relationships are mutual.

But you cannot build relationships with dozens of search consultants, nor would you want to even if you had time. Generally speaking, you want to work with no more than a handful of search consultants. To determine which firms, and which consultants within those firms, ask people you know and respect for the names of search consultants they admire and have worked with. Check out web sites for published articles and other information, including client ratings, of local consultants.

Having gotten the names of consultants and, hopefully, some introductions to them as well, use your own due diligence with potential search consultants. To get an idea of this person, ask how long he or she has been in the search business and about his or her business background prior to search, educational credentials, and clients and recent placements. How this person handles phone calls and face-to-face meetings will give you a good idea of whether the chemistry and respect are there for a good working partnership. If not, move on.

Strategy 3: Ads

Ads are another place where job seekers go wrong, especially online ads. It is very easy to respond to a lot of ads in a very short time, producing a euphoric sense of productivity. Particularly with the Internet, it can take little time to respond to an ad. In fact, in many cases, job seekers don't even bother with cover letters (a big no-no);

instead, with a keystroke, they simply send off a resume in response to an ad.

The problem with this approach is the opportunity cost: time better and more profitably spent in other ways. Here are some tips for maximizing the effectiveness of ads:

- Respond only to ads with a 70 percent or more fit with your background and skills.

- Research the company's situation and needs (Appendix E contains many online and print sources); in addition, your current employer's sales department is likely to have a corporate subscription to www.hoovers.com, so you can order detailed reports on companies and executives.

- Look at insider comments and other information about companies and executives; such web sites as www.vault.com, www.wetfeet.com, and www.infirmation.com (legal only) can all provide useful information.

- Use ads to identify who is hiring, the job description and qualifications, and the language they include; even if the location or employer is undesirable, the ads can provide useful information for your own cover letters and market research.

- If the ad lists a phone number or contact person, call to gather more information.

- Work your network to get to people in the company to gather more information and, ideally, an introduction to the hiring manager or other people in the know.

- Do not send a letter until your personal contact and research efforts are complete.

- With your resume, always send a cover letter detailing your competitive advantages, whether by snail mail or e-mail, demonstrating value to the employer in quantitative and relevant terms.

- Wait a few days after an ad appears to send your letter and resume (to avoid being in the initial influx of applications).

Strategy 4: Research and Direct Approach to Prospective Employers

The fourth strategy is to identify employers of interest, defined by criteria you deem relevant (industry, geographic location, size, product line or services, or whatever combination of factors are important to you). Refer to Appendix E for information sources to identify and research targets, such as Business Index ASAP, Reference United States, and Hoovers.

Published lists (e.g., Fortune's List of Most Admired Companies, 100 Fastest Growing Companies) are useful. Finally, the local version of the *Business Journal* is an excellent source of information on local companies, industries, and executives, and includes a list in each weekly issue (Top 25 Engineering Firms, etc.) that is compiled into an annual *Book of Lists*. All this information is useful for quick-and-dirty research to identify target employers. Check www.bizjournals.com for the web site.

Having identified and researched these companies, the next step is to gather additional information and possibly introductions through your network. If you cannot find any contacts to network your way into the company, the last resort is to send an unsolicited competitive advantage letter to the chair or CEO of the company.

How to Research and Reach Executives

Your network doesn't always provide access to the people you need to reach, nor can you always locate people who have been part of your network. But all is not lost. With ingenuity and online and print information resources, you can often identify the information you need: a name, phone number, e-mail address—using many alternatives, such as the following:

• Internet searches on executives, using search engines such as Google and Ask. For example, check Google for the executive's name (use the name of the company, too, if the executive has a common name) and a list of information, such as conference presentations, papers, board memberships, and possibly even an e-mail address. Check the web site www.theyrule.net to find board memberships and links between executives on different boards.

• Published sources such as D&B's *Reference Book of Corporate Management* and the *Directors and Executives* volume of *Standard & Poor's Register of Corporations* to identify corporate officers and directors. Short biographies include information on schools, degrees, and board memberships. This information is useful for making contact directly or through your network.

For example, if you find an executive got her MBA from Stanford and you, too, are a Stanford MBA or know someone who is, you may have established a point of contact. If an executive sits on a particular board, go to that organization's web site and look for the names of all board members for someone you or a colleague may know. The possibilities for contacts are expanded.

• Print or online subscriber sources such as the *Yellow Books* series. Produced by Leadership Directories, Inc. (www.leadershipdirectories .com), this series provides information (such as names, titles, and contact information) on leaders in corporations, government, nonprofits, and associations, among others. These include the *Corporate Yellow Book* (names, titles, and contact information for thousands of corporate officers of public and private companies, as well as lists of board members and their outside affiliations), *Law Firms Yellow Book*, and the *Associations Yellow Book*.

• Martindale-Hubbell for online and print directories of law firms and over one million lawyers in 160 countries, including biographical and practice information. The Lawyer Locater function at www.martindale.com allows you to search free of charge for a lawyer by name, firm name, geographic location, practice area, firm size, and more.

• The Association of Corporate Counsel's membership directory is searchable by attorney name or organization and provides law school, title, and contact information, including e-mail address.

• *CorpTech Directory of Technology Companies.* Available in print and through a subscriber database (www.corptech.com), the directory provides brief company profiles and names and titles of more than 250,000 high-technology executives.

- A national database of more than one million nonprofits (www.guidestar.org), includes names of executives and board members. Basic level of service is free, more advanced levels of information are by subscription.

- Internet databases such as Fortune, Forbes, BusinessWeek, and the Wall Street Journal. Use their search function to research executives and their companies.

- Internet people finder sites. Find street and e-mail addresses and phone numbers for executives and companies at www.switchboard .com, www.411.com, and www.whowhere.com.

- Business Index ASAP online database for references to management presentations to industry or trade conferences. Presentations can help you learn about individual style, corporate culture, and company vision and language so you can tailor your approach; conference lists of speakers can also provide opportunities to hear a target executive or someone from a target company speak and perhaps even have a chance for a one-on-one conversation.

- Company web sites. Many provide information on executives and links to articles on them.

- Online and print directories from your undergraduate and graduate educational institutions. These often list alumni by geographic location and employer, providing easy access to people you want to contact. Career services and alumni magazines are also useful resources.

- E-mail addresses. Try different variations on an executive's name and standard company e-mail formats (such as FirstName.LastName @Company; e.g., Jack.Smith@CompanyX.com or FirstInitialLastName @Company or FirstName_LastName@Company) or check the company's web site directly to find the standard company e-mail format. Be very careful about sending unsolicited e-mail to people you don't know. Many executives don't like it, see it as spam, won't read it, or worse, will consider you a pest. If you do use it, offer the recipient something, like a good idea or some useful information, along with your request.

It's all in the details—from whom you contact, to how you contact them, to what you ask. Most executives know the basic strategies—personal contacts, ads, recruiters, direct contacts with employers—but few know how to get the best results from them. The difference in impact is enormous.

And few know the online networking strategy that follows, much less how it can be used to streamline contact identification and professional networking.

Strategy 5: Online Networking

A fifth and newer strategy, online networking, is an outgrowth of the success of social networking sites such as Friendster. Business-focused online networking sites, such as www.linkedin.com, www .ryze.com, www.zerodegrees.com, and www.ecademy.com, are one of the fastest growing categories of web sites. The rules and functionality of the sites vary, but their shared focus is on building professional networks for information, introductions, business partners, candidates, deals, services, and jobs.

Sites such as LinkedIn and Ryze provide commercial applications of the "six degrees of separation" principle: that any person can be connected to anyone else through six intervening contacts. Connecting your online network with those of others accelerates the six degrees of separation.

By offering invitations to trusted colleagues and friends, who in turn invite their own trusted contacts to join, people create professional networks that grow exponentially and are of high quality. It also increases your professional and brand visibility rapidly and at minimal cost. In fact, one acquaintance focused his entire job search on online networking with his Harvard Business School colleagues and their networks.

Most people join these online networks by invitations from an existing contact, which immediately links them to their contact's network. You can also choose to join on your own and then invite your contacts to join your network, while also looking to connect with network members you already know. Join one or two of these networking sites as part of the job search process.

Why? Online networking represents the convergence of offline networking and Internet-based direct targeting strategies. It is both a form of networking, with much the same rules as the standard networking process described earlier in this chapter, and a process for streamlining contact development and targeting. The Internet has tapped the power of networks in previously impossible ways, both as a strategy to update your contact list and information quickly and as a way to quickly and easily link you with the networks of your network.

Instead of making calls or sending e-mails to update your contact list, you can send e-mail invitations to join the online network, simultaneously accomplishing the tasks of updating contact information and building your network as efficiently as possible. At the same time, you quickly update contacts on what you've done via your user profile.

Rules for Proper and Effective Use of Online Networking

• *Invest in the online network.* Write a thorough and richly detailed member profile. This is your business resume and your face to the online world. It deserves careful attention, not a cursory effort. Define your unique value proposition; your competitive advantages can help here. A sketchy profile can signal a one-sided investment in the network: a focus on what you can get out of the network but a bare minimum of data to help others. The inadvertent lack of reciprocity is discourteous as well as ineffective for making the most out of online networking.

Similarly, write a customized invitation to your contacts that spells out the value they can derive from participation in the network. Otherwise, your contacts may be puzzled by the invitation and less likely to join.

Part of your investment in the network is a commitment to respond promptly to requests from others. Even if you decline to fulfill the request, say so quickly.

• *Stick to trusted contacts to ensure and maintain your network's high caliber.* Sending invitations to people you don't respect or trust, or people you don't even know but would like to, erodes the quality and foundational trust of the network. In the case of people you don't know, it is akin to spamming them.

• *Make clear requests.* Just as with any offline requests in standard networking, clarity and specificity are more likely to generate the desired information or action. Have a purpose: Make very specific requests (for information, a meeting, or an introduction) that must often be passed on by an intervening contact. The more specific the request, the greater likelihood of getting a response from a distant connection.

Don't let the greater anonymity of an online contact lead you to ask for one thing only to misuse the contact for something else. The offline analogue is asking for an interview with a contact to gather information and then using the meeting to ask for a job. Do not compromise the trust of your contacts with shady behavior.

• *Reciprocate.* Reciprocity is the key to good relationships, online and offline. A viable network is more than the list of people in your Rolodex. Networking relies in part on the importance of greater diversity in your network: You increase your reach exponentially by connecting with people and their networks, rather than confining yourself to a limited number of contacts who all know each other. Occupying a central position in your network is also important because to the degree that you connect people with others, you occupy a more important place in the network.

By serving as a broker and offering to make introductions or connections for your contacts and their contacts, you demonstrate the principle of reciprocity at its best: Help others first.

Look for what you can do or offer, how you can serve your network by assisting others. Offer to write endorsements for people you respect (you can ask for them, too). Give away knowledge without asking or even expecting something in return. It is the right thing to do, and it has the added benefit of making your job-related networking much easier because it eliminates that uncomfortable feeling of needing something from others. In this me-first world, reciprocity is both the right and the effective thing to do. Remember that networking is fundamentally about relationships, not simply transactions to advance your career.

• *Mix online and face-to-face networking.* Online networking can serve an important purpose in your job search efforts and in your business career more generally, but it's important to remember that though online sites are good places for making contacts, a network is about relationships, not just contacts. Get out from behind the safety of your computer and meet with people to derive the full benefit from your network.

Using all five job search strategies will ensure that you optimize the results of your job search efforts, using a mix of high-tech and low-tech tools and specific ways to apply them effectively to get the best results.

Chapter 26

Make Proper Use of the Internet

Secret: Use the Internet for information, not jobs.

Ads have always been an overrated job search strategy, accounting for around 10 percent of executive jobs. Ads generate a lot of attention but relatively little in the way of jobs. The Internet provides a previously unimaginable resource for the job search, but it can also become a vast wasteland of unproductive effort.

I cannot tell you how many hours executives waste surfing the Internet daily, looking for the job of their dreams: sending out resumes, talking to recruiters about nonexistent jobs that were listed simply to locate promising candidates or talking to recruiters who see their resumes and talk to them about opportunities they aren't even handling, and interviewing by phone about opportunities that never materialize or never even existed. They feel safe and productive behind their computers, but this practice can be deadly to their search efforts.

Don't mistakenly fall into the black hole of Internet job search. For executives, the Internet can be a major time waster, a source of little more than ads that go nowhere and endless screening interviews with recruiters. The vast majority of executive jobs come through personal contacts. By the time you have reached the executive level, it is more important than ever to use contacts to generate introductions, information, and offers. Ads are much less likely to be the source of the job of your dreams, and even when they are, contacts are essential for positioning yourself most effectively. Whether due to seniority, visibility, or maturity, your contacts become increasingly important as you move up the ladder.

Use the Internet primarily for its rich information on companies, executives, and industries, rather than for job leads. Don't ignore the Internet as a source of employment opportunities, but keep its place in perspective; checking a few sites once or twice a week is sufficient. Supplement the job listings that are not blind with networking to find personal introductions and an additional source of entrée into a company with a promising opportunity when you locate it on the Internet.

Refer to the resources in Appendix E to make proper use, not overuse, of the Internet.

Chapter 27

The Game Plan

Secret: Plan to save time and improve results in your search.

Planning time and activities is the centerpiece of an effective job search, maximizing the return on the time you spend. There are several tools and strategies to make the most of the time you spend on your search. Treat your search as your top priority and organize and manage your time and activities carefully. The amount of time you have for your search depends on whether you are currently employed. There is empirical evidence that the speed of finding a new job is directly linked to the number of hours you have devoted to your search.

Whatever your employment status, the goal is to maximize the number of hours and the efficiency of your time expenditure on the job search. What follows are tips on how to accomplish both objectives:

- Treat the job search as a job, with daily and weekly targets that are nonnegotiable (e.g., 15 to 20 calls a day, minimum).
- Develop a game plan to organize your approach (using the Job Search Game Plan Worksheet) and efforts.
- Create a weekly schedule with time blocked out for job search activities, including time outside of work hours for activities such as writing letters, doing online and library research, meeting with contacts and search consultants.

Job Search Game Plan Worksheet

Ads

(List print and online ads and web sites you will check regularly.)

Search Firms and Employment Agencies

(List firms and contacts you will work with.)

Direct Targeting of Companies

(Identify target companies you will approach.)

Contacts

(List strategy and order of approach, if relevant, with different groups of your contacts, for example, contacts from professional associations, such as the New York City Bar Association. Call about openings in their organizations or contacts with other organizations.)

Online Networking Tools

(Identify professional networks you will use, such as LinkedIn, Ryze.)

Self-Introduction

(Write a 30-second telephone introduction of who you are, who referred you, what you are looking for, why you are qualified for this target job, and what you want from the person you are contacting.)

- Develop a manual or computer system for tracking contact information (name, address, phone, and e-mail, source of name, date of contact, outcome, follow-up date, etc.). Increasing numbers of my clients use computer spreadsheet databases to track contacts.
- Plan activity every day (minimum number of contacts or hours).
- Schedule in breaks.

- Get something from each contact (introductions, further contacts, etc.).
- Don't forget to exercise.
- If you are not currently employed, let friends and family know that you have a job—namely, finding a job—and let them know you are off-limits for calls and visits during work hours.
- If you are feeling discouraged, volunteer to help others in need, including other job seekers. Keep the search in focus—and in perspective.

Chapter 28

Track Your Progress

Secret: The successful job search is a process of incremental improvement, not big wins.

Continual performance improvement is imperative. Getting that top job is a job and one that demands constant vigilance and effort. You can't hope to win a top job if you are not performing at your best and constantly striving to improve your best performance. This requires constant tracking, measurement, and adjustment of your job search strategies to generate the best results.

Measurement is a key to job search success. Your ability to improve depends on collecting good performance data. Track your time, analyze your progress, and diagnose problems on a regular basis to constantly evaluate how you spend your job search time and what results you derive from each search strategy.

Your tracking system doesn't need to be elaborate to be effective. Record the amount of time you spend on each search strategy daily; periodically tabulate the time devoted and results from each strategy (number of return calls, meetings, interviews, second interviews, offers) to see where you're spending time and how it's working.

If you find that you are getting many initial interviews but no second interviews, this is a red flag to examine where your interview skills or approach may be at issue. If your e-mail approaches to contacts go unanswered, it may be worthwhile to experiment with phone calls or other strategies (e.g., a voicemail followed by an e-mail). Pay close attention to how you are spending time and what results you are getting so you don't use ineffective strategies for long.

The amount of time you devote to the job search, your target job and qualifications, and the strength of the job market are all variables that have a major impact on timing, but there are some benchmarks to note. For example, have you arranged face-to-face meetings within two weeks of launching your search (once the preparatory work of previous chapters is complete)? An interview within 30 to 90 days?

These checks can be an important diagnostic of what's working, what isn't working, and where your efforts are breaking down in the job search process. Remember that careful tracking and adjustments in strategies and emphases will do more to produce a successful outcome to your job search than the rare big win. Stop, measure, and evaluate to win the race.

Winning the race for your dream job is within your reach. Follow the steps and use the tools and strategies presented in these chapters to eliminate the stories and habits that are holding you back and to streamline your approach to defining what you want and pursuing it successfully. *Make the Right Career Move* will help you avoid costly mistakes and get the most from the limited time you can devote to your job search. The 28 critical insights and strategies will put you ahead of the competition, helping you develop the branding and positioning needed to stand out from the crowd. This book is designed to demystify executive job search and simultaneously provide you with a road map to success. It is simple but not easy.

Follow the advice contained in this book; it has helped hundreds of executives, attorneys, and other professionals make successful career moves. With focus, effort, and a sound strategy, your possibilities are unlimited. The job of your dreams is within your reach.

Appendix A

Using the Process to Find an Ideal Job

The story of a hypothetical executive, Joe Doe, whose case mirrors themes from many clients, demonstrates the steps to identify your individually ideal job. Joe was senior vice president of sales and marketing for a premier packaged goods company that was acquired by a global conglomerate. After 20 years with his employer and a stellar record of achievement, at the age of 45, Joe found himself looking for work and reconsidering his options.

Step 1: Assess Skills—What Are Your Greatest and Most Personally Enjoyable Skills?

Joe's greatest skills, as recorded on the Skills Inventory Worksheet, fell into three major areas:

1. General management skills, particularly allocating resources, budgeting, developing staff, motivating, and making decisions.
2. Functional sales and marketing skills, especially developing new product ideas, market research, and closing a sale.
3. Miscellaneous skills from the remaining categories of the Skills Inventory Worksheet, including writing, project planning and control, and proficiency with sales projection software.

Joe reported the highest levels of skill in all these areas, but he didn't enjoy using all of them equally. When he reviewed this list on the Summary page of the worksheet, he reaffirmed that he was good at all these things, but what he really loved to do above all was develop and motivate staff, be the point person who made the crucial decisions in sales and marketing, do market research, and develop new product ideas.

He was great at allocating resources, budgeting, project planning, and using sales software, but he considered these things necessary but uninspiring parts of the job. These were not the things that got and kept him passionate about sales and marketing for so many years.

Joe analyzed his top skills, as well as his areas of knowledge (branding, proficiency in French, and Miller Heiman sales strategies) and his personal strengths (chiefly, achieving results, making decisions, and remaining calm under pressure). French and Miller Heiman sales strategies were enjoyable but not essential parts of an ideal job. Similarly, his three greatest personal strengths were too general to define an ideal job, but Joe realized that achieving certain kinds of results, namely, creating new products or brands, was a critical part of what he loved to do.

As Joe evaluated branding and achieving results, the things that stood out were that he was a creative guy, a guy who led and inspired others, and made decisions based on his ability to come up with new product ideas and brand extensions. Market research and branding strategies were mere vehicles to a central skill: developing product ideas. Developing product ideas was an area of expertise and enjoyment and belonged in any description of an ideal job for Joe.

A second area of expertise and enjoyment essential to an ideal job was people management. Developing people and achieving results through people were both areas of great satisfaction and achievement for Joe. They, too, belonged on his final list. He realized that his emphasis on staff development was crucial to the development of team loyalty and motivation. Developing people stayed on the list; motivating people was eliminated.

Closing sales and writing were ways to express and apply his creativity and belonged in his final list of five top skills: developing product ideas, developing people, achieving results, closing sales, and writing.

Step 2: Assess Goals—What Are Your Primary Career, Relationship, and Personal Development Goals?

Using the Goal Planning Worksheet, Joe recorded his top goals in all three categories. After such a long time with his employer, Joe's career goals were more difficult to enumerate than relationship and personal development goals. Did he want another top sales and marketing job, or was now the time to move into a general management role, such as chief operating officer in a sales- and marketing-driven company? What were his long-term career goals?

Joe was just not sure. On the one hand, he could see himself as the CEO of a small entrepreneurial company in packaged goods; for years, he had been playing with ideas for a consumer product that would revolutionize the industry. But he feared that being the top guy would take him away from the creative product development challenges he relished, as well as from his teenagers and wife, who were tired of abbreviated family vacations.

Career goals he was sure of: to be elected to a board position with his industry's leading trade association and to write a book on innovative product development strategies. Because at this point he couldn't decide which of the larger career goals was more important, he included both: I want to be president of my own packaged goods company, and I want to be part of the executive team for a packaged goods leader known for being the best in sales and marketing.

Personal relationship goals included two family vacations a year, coaching his daughter's soccer team, and taking a couples course with his wife. Personal development goals included working out three to four times a week, running a marathon, improving his French, and learning Italian.

Prioritizing his goals, Joe realized that he was at a crucial juncture in his career and needed to put the two major career goals, running his own company and being part of a top executive team, on the priority list. Securing a board position in a major trade associa-tion would be an important advantage in fulfilling either of the major career directions. But he could also see that these three career goals potentially interfered with family vacations and running a marathon.

Joe realized that he could get the entire family involved in train-ing for and running a marathon; they were all athletic and had dis-cussed the idea in passing for years. This way he could meet relationship and personal goals at the same time. Joe was lucky; he might have had to finally conclude that family vacations rated higher priority than marathons, and that pursuing both goals was impossible in light of the need to make a major career transition to a demanding job as chief sales and marketing officer or chief execu-tive officer of another company. So he kept the marathon on the list and eliminated two annual family vacations. And in fact, making that career transition might mean scaling back all other goals, in-cluding the marathon, in the short term.

Step 3: Assess Satisfiers and Dissatisfiers— What Specific Aspects of Each Job Do You Like and Dislike Most?

Satisfiers and dissatisfiers differentiate the components of the ideal job more closely based on a careful evaluation of past job experi-ence. Joe recognized that the work that had interested him most in-volved situations in which the success of the company depended on a major product innovation or retooling. He also enjoyed leader and expert roles, and the results he enjoyed most were putting together the breakthrough product that saved the day, as leader of a highly motivated, high-performing team. He enjoyed seeing his people succeed and realize their own career goals.

Other major satisfiers were highly educated colleagues, a nonbu-reaucratic atmosphere where risk taking was encouraged, generous company programs in employee development and product research and development, a bias toward action, flexible hours, a management team that shared information openly, a fairly flat organizational structure, and innovative compensation programs. All these factors were listed on the Satisfiers and Dissatisfiers Worksheet.

Step 4: Record the Priority Skills, Goals, and Satisfiers and Dissatisfiers on the Ideal Job Factors Worksheet

With the information on skills, goals, and satisfiers, Joe was ready to complete the Ideal Job Factors Worksheet. Here is Joe's final list:

Skills: Developing product ideas, developing people, achieving results, closing sales, writing (5 skills)

Goals: Running my own company, being part of a top executive team, board position for trade association, and running a marathon (4 goals)

Satisfiers and dissatisfiers: Bet-the-company needs for products, leader role, expert role, developing breakthrough products, leading high-performance teams, seeing people realize career goals, highly educated colleagues, nonbureaucratic company, bias toward action, and innovative compensation programs (10 satisfiers)

Step 5: Consider Your Portfolio Career

Joe considered a series of breakthrough products or brands his most marketable accomplishments. These accomplishments made him attractive to competitors, to any consumer product company of any kind, to consulting firms—in fact, to any kind of organization in need of a strong product or identity. Another source of marketability was his revolutionary product idea, which could interest a venture capital fund. Or he could work for a VC himself, evaluating product ideas and business models of new ventures. The possibilities seemed endless when he looked beyond the competition.

Joe also pondered whether the ideal job factors he had identified suggested an alternative path to the more conventional corporate choices of another senior vice president (SVP) of sales and marketing or a top general management position. What about working for the International Olympics Organizing Committee? The advertising trades and the general media were speculating endlessly on the need for a new branding approach to marketing the Olympics after less than banner audiences for the past two Olympics. It would be a way to combine his love of branding and sports with his desire to do more community service. In addition, it would fill a gap in his portfolio of accomplishments and skills: the lack of nonprofit experience. This was a kind of experience he lacked but desired, because he eventually saw himself working in a nonprofit after his retirement from the private sector.

Or what about a less demanding corporate job so he could devote more time to developing his revolutionary new product idea, get funding and a patent—really make this an explicit part of his work, rather than something he mostly thought about in rare down times? Joe decided to put off final decisions on these alternative directions until he'd had a chance to narrow the ideal job factors further.

Step 6: Narrow the Ideal Job Factors

Joe reduced the ideal job factors to his top 10, using the forced ranking technique described in the Ranked Ideal Job Factors Worksheet to rank and record the top factors in order of importance. The top 10 were being part of a top executive team, running own company, developing breakthrough products, bet-the-company product needs, a board position with a trade association, leading high-performance teams, family vacations, running a marathon, a nonbureaucratic company, and a bias toward action.

The top factors reminded Joe that he was at a crucial juncture in his career. Seven of the 10 factors were specifically focused on major work roles and challenges, and yet they suggested no one clear direction. Leader or expert? Member or leader of an executive team?

Breakthrough products: hands-on or not? Do-or-die company situations as CEO or SVP of sales and marketing? It was time for the straw men.

Step 7: Identify and Evaluate Straw Men

Joe's final list of 10 top factors included both being head of a company and being part of a top management team, along with product ideas. He'd managed to reduce the list of factors to 10, but he still wasn't able to shake some of the other top factors from consideration. Coming up with straw men was a chance to put all this information to use. Joe used the Straw Men Worksheet to record and evaluate the straw men alternatives he generated.

What were at least three alternative employment directions to put his major factors to use? An obvious one was a top sales and marketing job at another company, perhaps a bigger, more prestigious company at a crucial growth stage, such as undergoing an essential product development or repositioning or need for a brand new sales and marketing strategy. But would that mean more bureaucracy and less action?

A second alternative was a general management role, perhaps in an up-and-coming company with a great product idea. That would be exciting, but making such a major transition to general management probably jeopardized the family goals of vacations and a marathon, as well as the professional goals of a board position and developing his revolutionary product idea. His kids wouldn't be at home that much longer, so it was hard to give up the family goals. He also realized that his great product idea had a limited shelf life; if he didn't pursue it soon, it was probably worthless.

The idea of a radically different direction, such as working for the Olympics or a venture capital fund or trying to secure VC funding for his product idea, all seemed a little too radical at this point in his career. A more service-oriented job seemed like a better fit in another 10 years, when the kids were out of college; he still had ample time to develop nonprofit experience. Heading a new venture to produce his product idea had all the risk of any new venture combined with the challenges of the top role—also not a good fit for his current need to maximize his earning power. And working in a VC would put him too far out of the action in product development and team development, both real loves of his.

Another straw man was a combination of the first two alternatives: working in the top sales and marketing role for a smaller, more entrepreneurial company, but one with a high-profile reputation for creativity. If the company was in need of developing a brand-new product category for the marketplace, it could maximize his ideal job factors. And it could potentially give him time to develop his product idea and obtain the board position while spending time with his family.

A final straw man alternative was that of consultant, working for a leading consulting firm to the consumer products industry or perhaps a leading branding firm. This had the intuitive appeal of lots of product challenges, teams, and industries. He could work with lots of blue-chip firms and increase his visibility.

Step 8: Select the Top Straw Man Scenario— Your Ideal Job Target

Here's what Joe determined. The traditional next step, a jump to a bigger version of his current job, was an obvious choice. His top factors and his definition of this target as necessitating major product, brand, and/or sales and marketing changes and creativity were a natural fit for his talents. His reputation as a leader and an expert in the field made him an attractive candidate and also leveraged some of the talents he most enjoyed. And some of the biggest companies in the field were known for major investments in R&D and in people, both also a fit with Joe.

The second straw man, an entrepreneurial alternative, was riskier, and as he considered it, he realized that after 20 years in a large company, with its infrastructure and resources, he would be more attracted to a top functional role rather than a general management role, at least as the next step. He recognized that part of his ability to be creative and make important decisions depended on an existing infrastructure to deliver quickly on his and his team's ideas and decisions.

In addition, he figured that in a smaller organization, he'd have a greater breadth to his role, including some larger operational responsibilities if he sought them, and he would. The idea of an entrepreneurial setting and perhaps being part of a team that created a whole new industry really excited him. The drawbacks were that the relative lack of infrastructure and resources would force him to assume more of the administrative roles, such as project management and budgeting, that he had been able to delegate to his team.

Finally, the consulting alternative was appealing because it would give him the opportunity to apply his creativity to multiple companies and industries rather than a single organization. The downside was that he wouldn't have the same staff development responsibilities he had always relished, though he recognized that some consulting firms might offer opportunities to develop and work with a specific team over the long term. He also wasn't sure that the consulting role would satisfy his desire to make decisions and get results; his ownership opportunities would not and could not be the same. Still, the sheer volume of creative opportunities and the chance to work with other experts in his field was enticing.

Formulating and evaluating the straw men alternatives helped Joe consider the set of important factors as a whole, identify areas where he needed more information to decide about an alternative, and reach greater clarity on his ideal job and next career move. His top choice? The top sales and marketing position in a smaller, more entrepreneurial, but high-profile consumer products company.

Action Verbs

This list of powerful verbs provides language to help you create strong accomplishment statements.

Did you discover something?

Detected	Found	Perceived	Solved
Determined	Identified	Proved	Uncovered
Diagnosed	Learned	Recognized	Verified
Discovered			

Did you observe or pay special attention to something?

Addressed	Inspected	Perceived	Surveyed
Examined	Investigated	Questioned	Tested
Experimented	Measured	Researched	Weighed
Explored	Observed	Studied	

Did you evaluate something?

Analyzed	Compared	Perceived	Rated
Appraised	Evaluated	Qualified	Reasoned
Assessed	Judged	Quantified	Reviewed

Did you understand something?

Attributed	Grasped	Perceived	Translated
Discerned	Interpreted	Transcribed	

Did you start something?

Activated	Created	Founded	Initiated
Adopted	Established	Generated	Instituted
Built	Formed	Implemented	Introduced

| Launched | Originated | Started | Undertook |
| Opened | | | |

Did you finish something?

Achieved	Concluded	Finalized	Reached
Accomplished	Ended	Finished	Realized
Attained	Established	Fulfilled	Terminated
Completed	Executed		

Did you document something?

Certified	Logged	Recorded	Supported
Charted	Mapped	Researched	Tabulated
Documented	Proved	Substantiated	

Did you supervise employees?

Appointed	Enforced	Hired	Referred
Awarded	Enlisted	Interviewed	Selected
Elected	Evaluated	Nominated	Staffed
Employed	Fired	Recruited	Terminated

Were you future oriented?

| Deterred | Forecast | Predicted | Projected |
| Estimated | Hypothesized | Prevented | Strategized |

Did you manage or lead?

Acted	Fostered	Led	Performed
Administered	Governed	Maintained	Piloted
Advised	Handled	Managed	Processed
Conducted	Headed	Motivated	Scheduled
Controlled	Influenced	Navigated	Showed
Directed	Integrated	Ordered	Supervised
Facilitated	Introduced	Oversaw	Used

Did you save the day?

Averted	Prevented	Saved	Succeeded
Diverted	Salvaged	Solved	Withstood
Prevailed			

Were you part of a team?

Advised	Conferred	Fostered	Participated
Aided	Consulted	Helped	Served
Assisted	Cooperated	Joined	Teamed with
Collaborated	Facilitated		

Did you obtain something new?

Acquired	Expanded	Purchased	Received
Bought	Obtained	Raised	Secured
Collected	Procured	Realized	Solicited
Cultivated	Produced		

Did you make something?

Assembled	Drew	Made	Programmed
Built	Engineered	Painted	Published
Composed	Fabricated	Photographed	Sketched
Constructed	Fashioned	Prepared	Used
Drafted	Formed	Produced	Worked

Did you provide something?

Dispensed	Generated	Presented	Responded
Distributed	Installed	Provided	Submitted
Fitted	Offered	Rendered	Supplied
Furnished	Performed		

Did you operate something?

Conducted	Fixed	Handled	Maintained
Controlled	Functioned	Implemented	Operated

Performed	Repaired	Troubleshot	Used
Ran	Tended	Turned around	Worked
Rebuilt			

Did you organize something?

Arranged	Combined	Coordinated	Prepared
Assembled	Compiled	Correlated	Structured
Categorized	Connected	Implemented	Summarized
Collected	Consolidated	Organized	Systematized

Did you make decisions?

Activated	Approved	Decided	Resolved
Adopted	Concluded	Determined	Settled

Were you responsible?

Assured	Ensured	Inspected	Satisfied
Confirmed	Guaranteed	Protected	Secured
Delivered	Guarded	Safeguarded	

Did you make changes?

Adapted	Extended	Reengineered	Structured
Adopted	Extracted	Refined	Supplemented
Centralized	Implemented	Reorganized	Systematized
Combined	Improved	Restored	Tailored
Consolidated	Improvised	Restructured	Unified
Converted	Introduced	Revised	United
Customized	Modified	Separated	
Edited	Reconstructed	Standardized	
Expanded	Redesigned	Streamlined	

Did you improve things?

Advanced	Corrected	Developed	Enlarged
Augmented	Cultivated	Enhanced	Enriched

Expedited	Increased	Revitalized	Treated
Extended	Modernized	Solved	Updated
Implemented	Reduced	Streamlined	Upgrated
Improved	Resolved	Surpassed	

Did you think up something new?

Conceived	Devised	Invented	Solved
Conceptualized	Discovered	Originated	Synergized
Created	Generated	Perceived	Synthesized
Designed	Improvised	Pioneered	Visualized
Developed	Innovated	Shaped	

Did you make connections?

Connected	Merged	Networked	Related
Matched			

Did you communicate something?

Communicated	Lectured	Recommended	Spoke
Demonstrated	Modeled	Related	Submitted
Displayed	Persuaded	Reported	Symbolized
Dramatized	Presented	Represented	Verbalized
Explained	Proposed	Shared	Wrote
Illustrated	Publicized	Showed	

Did you explain something?

Defined	Detailed	Elucidated	Explained

Did you negotiate?

Arbitrated	Intervened	Negotiated	Resolved
Balanced	Mediated	Reasoned	Settled
Brokered	Moderated	Reconciled	Solved

Did you save money, time, or resources?

Conserved	Economized	Minimized	Saved
Cut	Eliminated	Preserved	Trimmed
Decreased	Lowered	Reduced	

Did you work with people?

Advised	Influenced	Motivated	Reinforced
Coached	Informed	Persuaded	Served
Convinced	Inspired	Prescribed	Supported
Counseled	Instructed	Probed	Taught
Educated	Listened	Recommended	Trained
Facilitated	Mentored	Rehabilitated	Tutored
Guided			

Did you increase sales or territory?

Advanced	Enlarged	Grew	Publicized
Advertised	Expanded	Marketed	Sold
Developed	Extended	Opened up	Tripled
Doubled	Generated	Promoted	

Did you perform financial functions?

Analyzed	Checked	Divested	Merged
Audited	Collected	Financed	Reconciled
Balanced	Computed	Funded	Safeguarded
Budgeted	Dispensed	Invested	Solved
Calculated	Distributed	Liquidated	Took Public

Did you achieve something?

Accomplished	Attained	Gained	Realized
Achieved	Completed	Obtained	Secured
Acquired	Contributed	Reached	Surpassed

Did you receive honors or awards?

Acknowledged	Awarded	Elected	Nominated
Appointed	Credited	Granted	Selected
Assigned	Designated	Honored	Won

Did you get results?

Assured	Enabled	Influenced	Reinforced
Augmented	Ensured	Led to	Resulted In
Contributed	Facilitated	Promoted	Strengthened
Empowered	Furthered	Provided	

Appendix C

Sample Accomplishments

Please note that because page size is not 8½" × 11", like your resume, many accomplishments take more than two lines.

Sales, Marketing, and Account Executives

- Tripled sales volume to $40M in two years through product line extension and geographical expansion
- Developed company's top customer relationship with Wal-Mart, worth $4 million/year
- Closed $5M in the first year of a new geographic market, outpacing the rest of the United States and Europe
- Managed sales teams that consistently exceeded sales quotas by 20%
- Introduced a national accounts sales strategy and organization that reduced sales cost per new customer by 25%
- Turned 100% of a 50% hostile account portfolio throughout the Western region into revenue-producing accounts, receiving national award from company
- Consistently increased customer retention over 2% per year

Operations Executives

- Reversed a long-term volume decline and built gross revenues from $10M to over $32M in three years
- Selected as member of six-person nationwide team to develop five-year plan for food services, with estimated savings in excess of $15M

- Won formal recognition for consolidation of seven corporations into single entity, reducing prior $4M losses to $1M in year one of a three-year plan for profitability
- Led the merger integration team that identified $125M in savings
- Increased profits per partner an average of 10% for six consecutive years

Financial Executives

- Reduced preliminary acquisition bid by $10M through innovative value analysis that was accepted as basis for further negotiation
- Managed more than 30 due diligence reviews in connection with mergers, acquisitions, divestitures, and leveraged buyouts
- Structured an innovative off-balance-sheet transaction to reacquire a significant minority interest in NYSE company and simultaneously generate $70M in cash
- Accelerated year-end financial statement closing times by 50%

Biotech Executives

- Initiated and directed 15 academic collaborations with 10 institutions, generating over $1M of research at no outside cost to the company
- Raised $5M+ in start-up capital from VC and institutional investors as part of a two-person team
- Achieved protein expression levels from transduced primary cells up to 500-fold above levels previously reported
- Saved over $1M per year by establishing first computer database and centralized collection of plasmids, cultures, and cloning libraries
- Streamlined procedures on responses to outside requests for research materials that reduced turnaround from months to days

Business Development Executives

- Built a network of VCs to source quality deals aligned with corporate direction that accelerated deal flow by 25%

- Restructured joint venture with Fortune 50 telecom, increasing annual profits from break even to $700K within 10 months of assuming leadership

- Raised the initial $5M from the Silicon Valley's premier VC firm to fund what became the world's largest game software company, as member of six-person team

- Developed relationship management methodology that promoted cross selling on major accounts, increasing revenues an average of 20%

Law and Professional Service Firm Executives

- Improved revenue per lawyer 20% by bringing hourly rates in line with competitors' and accelerating fee inventory turnover

- Reduced costs over 20% in 2.5 years with no loss of productivity through staff reductions and aggressive landlord and vendor negotiations

- Decreased staff-to-attorney ratio 20% and reduced middle management staff 25% without disruptive layoffs

- Developed client management program, later adopted nationally, that helped reduce client defection rates 30% and contributed to five-year regional growth rate of 250%

- Championed program to improve cross-office collaboration that led to 20% increased market share in firm's top 10 clients

General Counsels

- Designed and managed corporate reorganization, effectively achieving tax-free status that increased net income more than 25%

- Eliminated roadblocks to $300M deal to merge six companies by creating corporate governance structure providing for balanced distribution of power

- Liquidated more than $15M of retail leases in poorly performing markets, obtaining settlements totaling less than 10% of exposure
- Negotiated strategic partnerships worth $150M with three media partners that enabled the company's rapid expansion into the animation industry

Chief Financial Officers

- Managed 35% growth over 24 months, resulting from opening 10 new facilities, completing five major remodels, and acquiring two real estate companies
- Produced the acquisition analysis and capitalization plan for the purchase of $200M regional competitor
- Raised $1.4M in public offering, completing SEC filings in record time
- Negotiated $8M line of credit and $5M capital equipment lease line

Information Technology Executives

- Developed an automated trading and quote access system for a financial services leader that generates $200M in annual revenue
- Drove $300M systems integration effort that delivered 15% savings in IT costs within the first six months and enabled corporate merger at record-setting speed
- Saved $1M a year through redesign of PC trading, quote, and portfolio management software enabling traders to perform their own brokerage tasks
- Introduced the first companywide change management and control system that decreased production failures by 35% without additional head count
- Completed two-year implementation of firmwide state-of-the-art PC-based LAN/WAN, meeting all time line milestones and budget goals

- Managed the development of industry's first real-time backup-trading systems, eliminating the need for a 20-person team to provide manual backup
- Saved $25M+ by renegotiating and integrating enterprisewide technology providers

Attorneys

- Obtained favorable judgment or dismissal in 90% of 50 cases in one year
- Recovered $8M in cash and securities through settlement of declaratory relief action involving joint venture with Mexico
- Originated and closed two manufacturing joint venture agreements in China, each requiring over 18 months of negotiations and six visits to China
- Coordinated successful defense of a leading health care chain against a series of 15 suits brought by competitors seeking billions of dollars in damages
- Designed "price-protection" warrant for mezzanine financing of cable company with unique provision for increased ownership percentage based on proposed IPO timing
- Managed successful $850M "bet the company" litigation for a Fortune 100 high-tech manufacturer against government allegations of misuse of corporate assets
- Closed a $7M preferred stock placement for an Internet start-up
- Averted potentially disastrous $90M claim against media start-up, settling for $50K
- Won four of five toxic tort trials for world's leading industrial chemical manufacturer
- Led attorney teams preparing series of 15 midmarket acquisitions over two years for a Fortune 500 financial institution
- Won largest case tried to jury in Illinois as part of three-person team, defeating a $3.5B demand, earning national recognition as one of U.S. top defense victories

- Achieved a favorable settlement of a hazardous waste case, avoiding $3M in potential penalties to a consumer product manufacturer

- Initiated legal evaluation of $2.5M strategic investment, later valued at $140M

- Negotiated and documented in Italian a $30M leveraged sale and leaseback of a vineyard and winery for a major Italian winery with a Fortune 500 conglomerate

- Saved major oil and gas company $15M in annual litigation and settlement costs by developing a litigation management plan for outside counsel

Health Care Executives

- Oversaw five multimillion-dollar capital improvement projects for a medical center, from planning through construction, completing all on budget and on time

- Conceived and implemented new emergency care service that became the regional market leader within two years

- Reduced average length of stay by one day by working with physicians and clinicians to modify practice patterns

- Recruited 15 established physician practices in 12 months as member of three-person search committee, increasing annual patient volume by 3,200 days

- Cofounded regional lab network that grew to 20 hospitals, leading to minimum annual savings per hospital of $100K

- Won commendation for Joint Commission on Accreditation of Healthcare Organizations survey, a result achieved by only 10% of hospitals in the nation

- Improved the relationship between the medical staff and management, which led to virtual elimination of physician complaints to the board within 60 days

- Won national award for health care leadership excellence twice in four years

Retail Executives

- Merged unprofitable catalogue division with mail-order division, achieving double-digit profits for five consecutive years
- Achieved 107% of last year sales, with 8 of 12 departments recording increases of up to 64% in recessionary retail market
- Directed expansion from 17 to 70 stores, including merger of an independent six-store chain
- Managed workforce that achieved first-ever bonus payout in the three years of the program
- Successfully coordinated the relocation and start-up of new 440,000 square foot distribution center, 90 miles away, with only three days of lost service to retail stores
- Developed standardized tracking system for all direct order stores to maximize inventory turns
- Generated the corporation's highest ready-to-wear profits and percent-to-total store volume
- Built online catalogue division, exceeding sales goals by 50% in the first 24 months

Human Resource Executives

- Introduced an online recruitment and staffing system that managed 50% increase in population and 40% reduction in cost during implementation
- Terminated 20+ long-tenured senior consultants with no lawsuits and no adverse publicity as part of a major downsizing
- Designed market-based compensation system with estimated 10-year savings of $20M
- Introduced a cafeteria-style plan that reduced benefits costs by 15% while increasing employee satisfaction with benefits options
- Built scalable HR programs that supported growth of new Internet company to 100 employees in the first nine months
- Created innovative recruitment and retention programs that kept attrition to under 30% of the industry average in a highly competitive market

Nonprofit Executives

- Led national mobilization to renew $750M federal legislation
- Developed and managed first zero-based operating budget, resulting in accurate revenue forecasts and timely and direct control of expenses
- Chaired national coalition during three appropriation campaigns that led to doubling of federal program funding, despite congressional efforts to reduce overall spending
- Introduced recruitment initiatives that increased racial and gender diversity by 25+% in city hires
- Oversaw preparation of comprehensive financial and fundraising plan to cover projected operating costs for new $100M museum
- Established referral relationships with 15 social service agencies to launch citywide expansion of emergency housing program, increasing client centers from 1 to 18

Corporate Communications and Public Relations Executives

- Developed the mission, business model, and organizational structure for strategic alliance partnerships worth $70M at launch of online media start-up
- Saved a $750K national consumer-brand account in first three weeks at agency by changing account staff and creating new program plans for five product managers
- Created turnkey publicity programs for 125 multistate brokerage offices, with more than 200% increase in media coverage
- Defused a reputational crisis resulting from initial media coverage of a bacterial outbreak at major clinic by serving as sole on-air and print media spokesman
- Directed advertising campaign selected as one of the "Best Campaigns of the Year" by *Apparel Magazine*
- Launched firm's first web site, winning national awards in three consecutive years and doubling the number of unsolicited inquiries

Appendix D

About the Resume

Resume Dos and Don'ts

Resume Dos

- Create a user-friendly document: lots of white space, short accomplishments, 12-point font, double space between accomplishment bullets, two pages maximum.
- Use short phrases set off with bullets for readability and impact.
- Print on ivory or white bond paper.
- Create only one version (customize cover letters, not resumes).
- Demonstrate value through results-oriented accomplishments and career summary.

Resume Don'ts

- Don't type dense fields of text.
- Don't write bullets that contain lengthy job descriptions or that mix job description with accomplishment.
- Don't include subjective or nonessential information, such as:
  —Personal characteristics (adjectives) in career summary.
  —Membership in groups irrelevant to building your case to your target audience.
  —Hobbies, interests, health, marital status, sex, age, number of children, height, weight.
  —Photos.
  —"References available on request."
  —Laundry list of areas of expertise.

- Don't include fancy graphics or layouts.
- Don't submit two-sided or multiple resumes.
- Don't use small margins and font size, packing too much information into two pages.
- Don't use company or industry jargon.
- Don't list career objectives that are very general or inapplicable.
- Don't offer outdated information, such as high school and college awards or honors, old jobs.
- Don't make declarations of value (versus demonstrations).
- Don't exceed two lines for accomplishment bullets, if at all possible.

Top 10 Executive Resume Mistakes

1. *Assuming a resume is unnecessary:* Even powerful, successful executives need the best resumes they can produce. Outstanding resumes open doors; get phone calls from recruiters, employers, and networking contacts returned; create buzz. Some experts downplay resumes in favor of "telling your story." Remember that for most executives, a great resume is the gatekeeper, allowing them to or preventing them from opportunities to tell their story. A great resume provides executives with the brand and the boost to pursue career moves confidently.

2. *Focusing too much on credentials rather than results:* There is always someone with more impressive credentials—bluer chip employers, bigger titles, better schools. Although employers look at these things, the way to stand out from the crowd is to show the results you've achieved through quantified accomplishments.

3. *Using a single strategy to generate accomplishments:* Executives like to produce results fast. When it comes to accomplishments, they stick to the easiest approach: listing their greatest accomplishments. But by ignoring the less obvious and more challenging approaches of using skills and areas of expertise to generate accomplishments, they sacrifice quality and positioning for speed. This compromises the marketing punch of the document that is the platform for career moves. Remember, this book promises *better* jobs faster, not just faster.

4. *Writing too much:* It's harder to be concise than to be verbose. Just because you did it, don't assume anyone else wants to read it. Make your resume no more than two pages and accomplishment bullets no more than two lines. When you've reached the executive suite, you likely have an extensive track record. A resume can represent only some of these accomplishments, so choose wisely and prune aggressively: it's very tough to limit a major accomplishment to one sentence when you know how much effort it entailed. But that's the kind of detail best kept

for an interview. Companies hire executives to cut to the chase. Your resume is the first chance to demonstrate this ability.

5. *Declaring value rather than demonstrating it:* Showcasing your track record depends on the use of accomplishments. Accomplishments do *not* speak for themselves. Quantification is essential to *showing* what you can do, *not* telling that you did it. In other words, don't tell the reader the sales campaign was innovative, tell the reader it won an industry award out of 200 competitors or led to a 10 percent sales gain in the first six months.

6. *Skipping the career summary:* Written like a good executive summary, a career summary provides a factual and powerful overview that hooks the reader, orients the reader to the nature and level of your experience and your particular expertise, and elicits a desire to read on. A generic career objective or career overview is a poor substitute because its generic nature, by definition, lacks specificity and punch.

7. *Overemphasizing job descriptions and mixing job descriptions and accomplishments in bullets:* Job descriptions provide important information about scope of responsibility, but keep them in perspective and in their proper place; a short paragraph following the job title and employer's name should suffice. Devote correspondingly more room to all-important accomplishments, and limit bullets to accomplishments rather than a mix of job description and accomplishment. These choices regarding focus and format simplify the reader's task, eliminating confusion by restricting bullets to results and creating a cleaner, clearer, and more reader-friendly document.

8. *Using a functional resume format:* A functional format organizes your accomplishments around topics, not jobs, and not necessarily the most meaningful topics to your audience of search consultants and prospective employers or even your contacts. This alternative format often confuses readers and arouses suspicion about what you are trying to hide by employing an alter-

native to the traditional chronological resume. Don't divert attention from your achievements by using a functional resume. The best alternative to the standard chronological format is a representative accomplishment format (see Chapter 10 for a discussion of resume format).

9. *Creating multiple resumes:* Writing more than one resume is a poor use of your time (see Chapter 12). Customize cover letters, not resumes.

10. *Settling for a good, not a great, resume: Make the Right Career Move* delineates a step-by-step process to achieve a powerful resume, not a quick-and-dirty one. Producing the best and most representative array of accomplishments using three strategies, whittling job descriptions and accomplishments to two pages without resorting to the problematic solutions of too-small margins and font size, eliminating company and industry jargon, and carefully selecting resume format and content to best showcase your track record are all steps worthy of your best and sustained efforts.

Guide to a Winning Resume

1. Gather information on job titles, years of employment, and employers; educational institutions, degrees, and credentials; and performance reviews.

2. Generate accomplishments using the three approaches (greatest, skill-based, and expertise-based accomplishments).

3. Formulate and quantify your accomplishments.

4. Decide on the resume format (chronological or representative accomplishments).

5. Draft the basic organization, beginning with identifying information.

6. Complete the Professional Experience section, writing job descriptions, followed by major accomplishments for each job in descending order of importance. Include a few words about each employer in the job description.

7. Complete the Education (and Credentials) section, listing dates, degrees, field or major, institutions, and locations.

8. Complete the Professional and Community Affiliations section only if you have important information to include.

9. Adjust the number, content, syntax, and mix of accomplishments to convey your unique contributions and style. Remember, the resume cannot exceed two pages.

10. Write the Career Summary once the text is finalized.

The Role of Information and Research in Your Job Search

Research and information gathering are central to the effectiveness of the five job search strategies. Fortunately, the information resources available to you are better than ever. But particularly with the vast but largely unevaluated resources of the World Wide Web, that's the good news *and* the bad news. How can you pick among the seemingly infinite resources to find a few good web sites and search tools? Because this book is designed to be a practical guide rather than an exhaustive reference guide, the suggestions that follow represent some recommendations based on the professional advice of information experts (librarians), along with my own practical experience with clients.

Getting Started

General Tips

- Emphasize contacts with people most, not information gathering. But gather information to enhance the effectiveness of each search strategy.
- Use validated sources to get the best results.
- Learn how to use information sources.
- Consult librarians for tips on tutorials and web sites.
- Use information as a tool, not an end in itself.

Web Tutorials

Some prominent university libraries and noncommercial sites provide tutorials and recommended Internet strategies and resources for the novice. For example:

- UC Berkeley Library provides an excellent online tutorial entitled "Finding Information on the Internet" and available at: http://www.lib.berkeley.edu/TeachingLib/Guides/Internet/Find Info.html.

  In simple but clear terms, this tutorial explains everything from the differences between the Internet and the Web to search strategies, how to evaluate web pages, and recommended search engines and subject directories.

- Guide to Effective Searching of the Internet, a tutorial located at http://www.brightplanet.com/deepcontent/tutorials/Search/index .asp that provides a simple introduction to how to structure information queries precisely and effectively.

- Researching Companies Online, a free business tutorial located at http://www.learnwebskills.com/company "presents a step-by-step process for finding free company and industry information on the World Wide Web." Topics include how to research an industry, how to research nonprofit organizations, and how to identify high-level company information.

Search Engines, Subject Directories, Virtual Libraries, and Portals

The Web is changing fast. Sites, search engines, subject directories, and other major information resources change, appear, and disappear with such rapidity that any statements or suggestions can be quickly outdated. Ref Desk (www.refdesk.com) describes the Internet as "the world's largest library . . . [with] everything . . . scattered about on the floor." It's no surprise, then, that search engines, subject directories, virtual libraries, and portals represent four different ways to make sense and use of the vast Internet resources. In addition, consult a reference librarian at your local public or university library for recommendations on classes or Internet tutorials on how to use the Web, as well as search engines and other Web resources.

In the early days of the Internet, there were two major classes of information sources on the Internet: search engines and subject directories. *Search engines* use computer programs to search parts of the Web contained in their databases, matching them with keywords that you enter. *Subject directories* are collections of web sites in a particular subject area that have been selected and categorized by human editors and thus validated; you specify by keyword your particular interest in a subject area and receive a list of sites from the directory that contains this word.

The distinctions between search engines and subject directories are blurring for commercial reasons as both aim to become one-stop shopping. For example, although Google began as a search engine, it now has links to a directory database organized by topic. Similarly, subject directories like Yahoo now include search engines.

In addition, there are *virtual libraries*, libraries that exist in electronic form, that may be thought of as general or specific subject directories, as they are constructed by humans and, in many cases, librarians.

Finally, *portals* represent another way to gather information, in this case in the form of a web site that provides a gateway to numerous links in one or more particular subjects.

Subject Directories

- www.yahoo.com: The best-known and most comprehensive subject directory with many broad categories.

Search Engines

- www.google.com: You know you're successful when the name of your company becomes a verb! Google is the most popular search engine, allowing the user to "google" or identify information on people and companies. Despite its large database and its justifiably excellent reputation for providing useful links, don't depend on it exclusively. Overlap studies by professional librarians (see UC Berkeley Library tutorial) show that approximately 50 percent of the searchable pages on any search engine are unique to that search engine. The conclusion? Always get a second opinion.

- www.ask.com: Ask Jeeves in an earlier incarnation, this search engine has been overhauled, renamed, and streamlined to very good effect. It provides an easy way to expand or narrow search results, has been decluttered of ads, and provides a handy column of useful search links (from encyclopedia to news) to refine your search results and a simple way to preview results without leaving the search page.

- www.alltheweb.com: A huge database, second only to Google (use advanced search function).

- www.altavista.com: A large database but not as large as Google or AlltheWeb. Links to www.smartpages.com to check the Yellow Pages or the White Pages for addresses and phone numbers of the person or company you are seeking.

- www.vivisimo.com: Unlike the preceding search engines, Vivisimo is a metasearch engine that indirectly searches three huge search engine databases simultaneously. Metasearch engines may sound like the best way to go, as they can search multiple databases, but they are only as good as the databases they search. This is a particularly good one.

- www.dogpile.com: Another good metasearch engine that provides an easy way to compare results from each search engine.

Virtual Libraries

- www.refdesk.com: Its web site proclaims, "The single best source for facts on the Net." And a good case can be made for this award-winning, comprehensive, noncommercial, and free web site with links to more than 20,000 sites. RefDesk was designed to help the user access and navigate the Internet. Check the site map for links to search engines, including Google and AlltheWeb, Internet guides and tutorials, major newspapers worldwide, new sites and recommended sites, a wide array of subject matter indexes and reference tools, desktop resources such as *Bartlett's Quotations* and the *Encyclopedia Britannica,* and thesaurus and dictionary searches. And don't forget RefDesk for inquiries and free search assistance.

- www.lii.org: The Librarians' Internet Index allows you to search and browse a subject directory of thousands of the best Internet resources organized into 14 main topics and hundreds of related topics. The information is vetted by professional librarians and organized to promote usability.

- www.ipl.org: The Internet Public Library was created by the University of Michigan School of Information and Library Studies as "the first public library of and for the Internet community." Subject collections include business, with links to business directories, business and economics news, and other subheadings. Within the subheadings, find useful, librarian-vetted links to web sites and other relevant resources. Also has an Ask a Question reference service.

Portals

The goal of the executive-oriented portal, CEOExpress (www .ceoexpress.com), is to identify, edit, organize, and link to the best Web resources for executives. Includes links to major national and international newspapers, business periodicals, newsfeeds, and publications; search engines and other Internet tools; business research information such as financial markets, quotes, SEC and government information, statistics; and office tools such as a currency calculator, essential software downloads, reference tools, and airline links. A premium version, CEOExpressSelect, is available by subscription only.

SearchSystems (www.SearchSystems.net) was created to link to more than 35,000 public records databases to conduct background research on companies. Search by type of database (e.g., "census"). Performs state, national, and international searches.

Business and Company Information

Background Information on Companies and Executives

- www.hoovers.com: Hoovers is a great resource for information on more than 16 million public companies and large private companies worldwide. Now owned by D&B, a longtime business information resource, Hoovers provides comprehensive company, industry, and market intelligence. Basic information on companies and executives is available free, but detailed reports are available for a fee and some involve a subscription.

- www.bizjournals.com: The online media division of American City Business Journals, which provides local business intelligence on 55 markets, from Albany to San Francisco, in weekly local newspapers such as the *San Francisco Business Times*. Excellent source of information on local companies, industries, and executives. Each issue includes a list (e.g., Top 50 Law Firms, Top 100 Public Companies) and all lists are compiled into an annual *Book of Lists*, which is a great resource for researching and contacting local employers. The company operates the web sites for each of the company's print journals.

- www.fortune.com Articles from *Fortune* magazine and famed Fortune lists, from the Fortune 500 to America's Most Admired Companies, are available online; some reports are available for purchase.

- www.forbes.com: Allows you to search the *Forbes* magazine archives for articles and to receive free e-mail newsletters on such topics as executive in the news, international business, and specific industries.

- www.leadershipdirectories.com: Publishes and sells 14 directories or Yellow Books that collectively comprise the Leadership Library, which lists 400,000 leaders of major U.S. business, government, professional, and nonprofit organizations. Available for purchase in print or electronic form. Provides titles, addresses, direct phone numbers, and e-mail addresses of executives.

- www.theyrule.net: Focuses on board members of major U.S. companies and interlocking board connections. Good way to research board directors and corporate power structures as well as identify possible contacts from within your network.

- www.linkedin.com, www.ryze.com, and www.ecademy.com: Among the newer Internet resources that can be used to identify and update your network, and identify contacts with target executives and organizations within your own network, providing a commercial application of the "six degrees of separation" networking principle that only six intervening contacts can connect any two people. (See the section on online networking in Chapter 25 for a more complete description.)

- Business Index ASAP and Business & Company Resource Center are among the online reference databases offered by Info-Trac. Both are available through library subscriptions at most large public libraries and academic libraries. Business Index ASAP is a database of several hundred periodicals, magazines, and select newspapers that provides instant access to full text and images in many cases. It offers a rich source of articles on companies and executives worldwide, as well as management topics and business theories and practices. Search by name of company and executive or subject area.

- Another InfoTrac database, Business & Company Resource Center, brings together company profiles, rankings, company histories, and information on executives. This database is searchable by company, officer, or director name.

- Reference United States is an online database on 12+ million U.S. businesses, from large public companies to small, privately owned businesses with one or two employees. Can search by executive name and/or title, company, or other descriptors. Its real strength is the ability to search by using various parameters, such as type of business, location, sales volume, number of employees, and SIC code. Good in coming up with target companies. Most large public libraries and academic libraries are subscribers.

- *Strauss's Handbook of Business Information* (2nd edition, 2004) is a useful print compendium of online and print business reference sources, including directories, periodicals, newspapers, statistics, and fields of business information.

Corporate Filings and Other Financial Information

- www.dnb.com: Order business and credit reports from Dun & Bradstreet's (now, D&B) business database that includes information on more than 100 million businesses worldwide (the world's largest business database). Despite having 90 percent of the Global 1,000 companies, 80 percent of D&B's U.S. businesses have 10 or fewer employees.
- www.10kwizard.com: Subscriber access to SEC filings, including 10Ks, quarterly and annual earnings reports filed with SEC. Includes ability to perform keyword searches on up-to-the-minute SEC filings. Hailed by *Money Magazine, Fortune,* and *BusinessWeek*.
- www.sec.gov: Free searches of SEC filings.

Finding Street and E-mail Addresses and Phone Numbers

- www.whowhere.com: Powered by Lycos, allows you to search for a person or a business.
- www.switchboard.com: Searches Internet-based yellow pages for companies and individuals.
- www.411.com: Internet searches of Yellow Pages and White Pages for individuals and companies.

- www.yell.com: Online yellow pages for U.K. businesses.

- www.europages.com: Lists phone numbers, addresses, and other company information for more than 600,000 companies in more than 35 European countries. Site may be viewed in more than 20 languages.

Insider Information on Companies

- www.vault.com: A career information site that provides extensive information on industries and companies, job search articles and guides (not targeted to executive audiences), and message boards (not sponsored by the target company) that provide insider postings for the preceding 60 days. Fee-based products include a series of books that rank industries, including the *Vault Guide to the Top 100 Law Firms*, *Vault Guide to the Top 50 Consulting Firms*, and the *Vault Guide to the Top 50 Banking Employers*. Other products include workplace surveys that are detailed accounts of what it's like to work at a specific employer; interview surveys that describe the hiring process; and interviews, salary surveys, and business outlook surveys that provide a competitive analysis of strengths and weaknesses. Check for availability at local libraries.

- www.wetfeet.com: A career web site that provides company interviews, company profiles, industry profiles, real people profiles, insider guides (for pay), and discussion boards about industries and specific careers. Much of the information and the guides are pitched for more junior employees but offer useful basic information nonetheless.

- www.infirmation.com: Part of FindLaw Career Center (www.careers.findlaw.com), this site provides capability to search for information on a law firm or to locate an attorney. Also contains GreedyAssociates (www.greedyassociates.com), with free e-mail newsletters, job postings, and message boards providing insider information and gossip on law firms across the country.

Useful Career and Job Web Sites

General Career Web Site

- www.rileyguide.com: A career web site that provides job and ca-reer resources as well as employment listings. The primary value for an executive job hunter is its well-edited list of links on exec-utive topics, particularly Executive Compensation & Severance, which is part of its Salary Guides section.

Compensation Information

- www.salary.com and www.SalaryExpert.com: Major providers of online salary data, including salary reports for executive posi-tions. These sites provide individual salary compensation esti-mates for your location and job, for a fee.

- www.dogpile.com (use advanced search function and enter name of position and "salaries"—for example, "attorney salaries"): Can be useful for getting salary survey information.

Employment Opportunities

- www.jobcentral.com: Employment search engine that allows you to search for jobs in the United States and directs you to the company or recruiter web site offering the job without having to go to another link. Includes executive and attorney positions. Lists openings by title, employer, and location.

- www.careers.wsj.com: Provides a nationwide database of job openings to search, along with a rich archive of articles written by career columnists and others on topics from salary negotia-tion to interviewing to maintaining work-life balance, and an individual salary calculator.

- www.craigslist.org: A grassroots phenomenon that started in the San Francisco Bay Area and spread across the country, Craigslist was described in a *Wall Street Journal* article as the favorite job search web site of major search firms. For the most part, the job listings are junior and rarely include executive listings. On the other hand, you can also post your resume. When I mentioned my disappointment at the listings to an executive client, he said, "It's not what's listed, it's who's reading that matters." Take a look.

- www.acca.com: Web site of the Association of Corporate Counsel, providing a list of in-house opportunities for lawyers.

- www.attorneyjobs.com and www.lawcrossings.com: Large online databases of jobs for attorneys by subscription.

- www.occupationpro.com: A large online database of legal positions with large and small firms, in-house positions with companies, and judicial clerkships.

- ExecuNet, a paid membership web site with job postings and networking for executives making $100,000 and above. Web site lists positive statements from *BusinessWeek*, *Forbes*, and *Fortune*.

- www.netshare.com: Another web site for $100,000+ executives, requiring paid subscription and providing job listings from recruiters and employers. "Best site" endorsements from *Forbes* and *Fortune*.

- www.ritesite.com: For an annual fee, provides access to the listings of more than 500 executive search firms across the country. Option to post your resume anonymously.

- www.futurestep.com: A Korn/Ferry International company, provides assessment and recruitment of middle to senior management positions, accessing candidates from its web site.

Consulting and Independent Contractor Opportunities

- www.msquared.com: Major independent broker of independent consultants. Provides high-level project-based contractors to companies around the country and globe. Contractors have an average of 15 years of experience and come from all functions. M-Squared is interested in people who are looking for contracting positions on an ongoing basis rather than as interim steps between jobs.

Worksheets

List of Stories Worksheet

- **Story #1:**

- **Story #2:**

- **Story #3:**

- **Story #4:**

- **Story #5:**

- **Story #6:**

- **Story #7:**

- **Story #8:**

- **Story #9:**

Cost/Benefit Analysis Worksheet

Story	Costs	Benefits	Steps to Give It Up

Possibilities Worksheet

Event or Activity	Why Did You Enjoy It?
Work #1:	
Work #2:	
Work #3:	
Extracurricular #1:	
Extracurricular #2:	
Adolescent #1:	
Adolescent #2:	
Childhood #1:	
Childhood #2:	

Skills Inventory Worksheet

The first step in the job search process is to determine where you are now. There are three kinds of attributes you will assess:

- Skills: What you can do (e.g., write, analyze, program, sell)
- Knowledge: What you know about or know how to do
- Personal Strengths: Characteristics unique to you (e.g., creative, cooperative, motivated, energetic)

A. Review the lists of SKILLS, KNOWLEDGE, and PERSONAL STRENGTHS on the following pages.
B. Make a cross in the box that best describes your level of proficiency using the following scale:
   1 = Basic: general working knowledge of concepts, policies, procedures, or practices
   2 = Intermediate: full working knowledge of concepts, policies, procedures, or practices
   3 = Advanced: detailed knowledge of concepts, policies, procedures, or practices
C. Include additional attributes you have that are not listed.
D. Leave blank attributes with which you are unfamiliar or that you feel you don't have.
E. Record all ratings of 3 (Advanced) on the Summary page.
F. Circle all items on the Summary page that you enjoy using. These are your priority skills, areas of knowledge, and personal strengths.

SKILLS

1 = Basic
2 = Intermediate
3 = Advanced

Supervision/Management

1 2 3
___ ___ ___ Allocating resources
___ ___ ___ Analyzing/assessing
___ ___ ___ Balancing business and staff needs
___ ___ ___ Budgeting
___ ___ ___ Communicating relevant information
___ ___ ___ Counseling/coaching
___ ___ ___ Delegating
___ ___ ___ Developing staff

1 2 3
___ ___ ___ Directing others
___ ___ ___ Hiring staff
___ ___ ___ Implementing changes
___ ___ ___ Implementing policies
___ ___ ___ Initiating action
___ ___ ___ Integrating company objectives
___ ___ ___ Interviewing
___ ___ ___ Leading meetings
___ ___ ___ Making decisions

(continued)

Skills Inventory Worksheet (*Continued*)

1 2 3
___ ___ ___ Managing staff performance
___ ___ ___ Monitoring productivity
___ ___ ___ Motivating
___ ___ ___ Negotiating
___ ___ ___ Organizing/coordinating
___ ___ ___ Planning
___ ___ ___ Public speaking
___ ___ ___ Scheduling
___ ___ ___ Selecting staff/planning staffing needs

1 2 3
___ ___ ___ Solving problems
___ ___ ___ Strategizing
___ ___ ___ Time management
___ ___ ___ Writing performance plans/reviews
___ ___ ___ Writing proposals
___ ___ ___ _____
___ ___ ___ _____
___ ___ ___ _____

Communication

1 2 3
___ ___ ___ Composing correspondence/written material
___ ___ ___ Defining
___ ___ ___ Describing
___ ___ ___ Drawing/illustrating
___ ___ ___ Editing
___ ___ ___ Explaining
___ ___ ___ Expressing yourself clearly
___ ___ ___ Interpreting
___ ___ ___ Listening effectively
___ ___ ___ Proofreading

1 2 3
___ ___ ___ Public speaking
___ ___ ___ Publicizing
___ ___ ___ Reporting
___ ___ ___ Responding to inquiries
___ ___ ___ Spelling
___ ___ ___ Teaching/training others
___ ___ ___ Using correct grammar
___ ___ ___ Writing clearly
___ ___ ___ _____
___ ___ ___ _____
___ ___ ___ _____

Customer Relations

1 2 3
___ ___ ___ Being courteous
___ ___ ___ Being tactful/diplomatic
___ ___ ___ Building rapport
___ ___ ___ Calming irate customers
___ ___ ___ Determining customer needs
___ ___ ___ Expressing yourself clearly
___ ___ ___ Following through on communications
___ ___ ___ Listening effectively
___ ___ ___ Promoting firm's image

1 2 3
___ ___ ___ Promoting firm's products and services
___ ___ ___ Remembering and using customers' names
___ ___ ___ Resolving problems
___ ___ ___ Responding to inquiries
___ ___ ___ Using effective telephone techniques
___ ___ ___ _____
___ ___ ___ _____
___ ___ ___ _____

Skills Inventory Worksheet *(Continued)*

Financial/Mathematical

1 2 3
__ __ __ Analyzing/assessing
__ __ __ Auditing
__ __ __ Calculating
__ __ __ Comparing
__ __ __ Computing
__ __ __ Evaluating

1 2 3
__ __ __ Problem solving
__ __ __ Projecting
__ __ __ _____
__ __ __ _____
__ __ __ _____

Research/Analytical

1 2 3
__ __ __ Analyzing/assessing
data/statistics
__ __ __ Classifying
__ __ __ Compiling data
__ __ __ Documenting
__ __ __ Evaluating
__ __ __ Hypothesizing
__ __ __ Investigating

1 2 3
__ __ __ Monitoring
__ __ __ Organizing/coordinating
__ __ __ Problem solving
__ __ __ Researching
__ __ __ Systematizing
__ __ __ _____
__ __ __ _____
__ __ __ _____

Sales/Marketing

1 2 3
__ __ __ Analyzing/assessing
customers' needs
__ __ __ Asking probing questions
__ __ __ Closing a sale
__ __ __ Describing product
features
__ __ __ Developing new product
ideas
__ __ __ Evaluating
__ __ __ Managing client portfolios
__ __ __ Market planning

1 2 3
__ __ __ Market research
__ __ __ Marketing/direct response
__ __ __ Meeting quotas
__ __ __ Negotiating
__ __ __ Organizing/coordinating
__ __ __ Overcoming objections
__ __ __ Selling benefits of products
__ __ __ Setting goals/objectives
__ __ __ _____
__ __ __ _____
__ __ __ _____

(continued)

Data Processing/Systems

1 2 3

__ __ __ Analyzing application
systems

__ __ __ Analyzing operating
systems and hardware

__ __ __ Capacity planning

__ __ __ Creating systems
specifications

__ __ __ Designing databases

__ __ __ Modifying package
software

__ __ __ Monitoring vendors

__ __ __ Programming languages
and methods

__ __ __ Project planning and
control

__ __ __ Providing product
support/user liaison

1 2 3

__ __ __ Quality control

__ __ __ Security planning

__ __ __ Structured analysis

__ __ __ Structured design

__ __ __ Structured tests

__ __ __ Systems programming

__ __ __ Technical writing: systems
documentation

__ __ __ Technical writing: user
training/tutorials

__ __ __ _____

__ __ __ _____

__ __ __ _____

__ __ __ _____

Personal Computers

Use the blank spaces to list specific packages you are familiar with.

1 2 3 Database package

__ __ __ _____

__ __ __ _____

__ __ __ _____

1 2 3 Integrated packages (e.g.,
Lotus 123)

__ __ __ _____

__ __ __ _____

__ __ __ _____

1 2 3 Electronic spreadsheets

__ __ __ _____

__ __ __ _____

__ __ __ _____

1 2 3 Word processing packages

__ __ __ _____

__ __ __ _____

__ __ __ _____

Skills Inventory Worksheet *(Continued)*

KNOWLEDGE

Because each manager has acquired a unique body of knowledge, you must choose, enumerate, and evaluate what you know.

Examples of knowledge you might list are:

Foreign language fluency
Real estate law
Benefits planning
Computer languages

1 = Basic
2 = Intermediate
3 = Advanced

1 2 3

— — — _____

— — — _____

— — — _____

— — — _____

— — — _____

— — — _____

— — — _____

— — — _____

— — — _____

— — — _____

(continued)

PERSONAL STRENGTHS

1 = Basic
2 = Intermediate
3 = Advanced

1 2 3

___ Accepting supervision
___ Achieving goals/results
___ Being cooperative
___ Being dependable
___ Being diplomatic
___ Being discreet
___ Being flexible
___ Being impartial
___ Being objective
___ Being patient
___ Being resourceful
___ Being tactful
___ Being tolerant
___ Building rapport
___ Compromising
___ Contributing ideas
___ Evaluating alternatives

1 2 3

___ Following through on commitments
___ Gaining cooperation of others
___ Inspiring confidence
___ Making decisions
___ Managing time
___ Motivating others
___ Persuading and influencing others
___ Remaining calm under pressure
___ Setting priorities
___ _____
___ _____
___ _____

Skills Inventory Worksheet (*Continued*)

SUMMARY

Now that you have taken inventory of your skills, summarize the information. Record your greatest skills, bodies of knowledge, and personal strengths (Level 3) on this sheet. Circle those that you most enjoy using.

Skills: _____   _____

_____   _____

_____   _____

_____   _____

_____   _____

Knowledge: _____   _____

_____   _____

_____   _____

_____   _____

_____   _____

Personal Strengths: _____   _____

_____   _____

_____   _____

_____   _____

_____   _____

Goal Planning Worksheet

List your primary goals in each of three areas: career, relationships, and personal development.

What is your conception of the ideal attainments in your **CAREER?** Be as free and specific as possible in selecting these goals. Summarize them below.

Examples: I want to become president of my own company.

I want to sit on the board of a Fortune 500 company.

I want to be recognized as an expert in the financial services industry.

I want to lead project teams managing major system conversions.

1.

2.

3.

4.

What is your conception of ideal attainments in your **PERSONAL RELATIONSHIPS?** Be as free as possible in selecting these goals. Summarize below.

Examples: I want to spend nights and weekends with my family.

I want children.

I want to coach my daughter's soccer team.

1.

2.

3.

4.

Goal Planning Worksheet *(Continued)*

What is your conception of ideal attainments in your **PERSONAL DEVELOPMENT AND LEARNING?** Be as free as possible in selecting these goals. Summarize below.

Examples: I want to learn to fly an airplane.

I want to practice yoga.

I want to exercise three times a week.

I want to learn Spanish.

1.

2.

3.

4.

GOAL PRIORITIES: Select the goals from the three previous items that seem most important to you at this time. Do not choose more than four. Rank-order them in terms of importance, with 1 being the most important.

1.

2.

3.

4.

POTENTIAL GOAL CONFLICTS AND DEPENDENCIES: One of the major deterrents to goal accomplishment is conflict between goals. The person who ignores the potential conflicts between job and family, for example, will probably end up abandoning goals because of the either/or nature of many decisions. In some cases, working on one goal can help you reach another goal (goal dependencies). For example, learning to windsurf (a personal development goal) may facilitate increasing your network of friends (a relationship goal). List the goal conflicts and positive goal dependencies below.

(continued)

Goal Planning Worksheet *(Continued)*

GOAL CONFLICTS

1.

2.

3.

GOAL DEPENDENCIES

1.

2.

3.

IMPLICATIONS FOR ACTION: What are the implications for career planning and management of your goal priorities, conflicts, and dependencies (e.g., a job that requires limited travel so you can spend nights and weekends with family)?

1.

2.

3.

Satisfiers and Dissatisfiers Worksheet

Analyze current and prior jobs carefully for the specific things you found particularly satisfying and dissatisfying. Although these factors are highly variable, the following questions may suggest some sources of satisfaction and dissatisfaction. There is no limit to the number of items you list. Use additional pages if necessary.

- What work interests you most and makes best use of your skills (specific projects, activities, organizational or job challenges)?

- What kinds of results are most meaningful to you?

- What roles do you enjoy most?

- What kinds of rewards matter most to you?

- What kind of people do you enjoy as colleagues and clients?

- What work setting is ideal?

- What is your preferred geographic location?

- What other factors have had a make-or-break impact on your satisfaction in each job?

Ideal Job Factors Worksheet

Skills: What are your greatest and most enjoyable skills? List up to 5.

1.

2.

3.

4.

5.

Goals: What are your top career, relationship, and personal development goals? List up to 4.

1.

2.

3.

4.

Satisfiers and Dissatisfiers: What specific aspects of your job, work setting or culture, colleagues, or work situation are most satisfying and dissatisfying? List up to 10.

1.

2.

3.

4.

5.

6.

7.

8.

9.

10.

Ranked Ideal Job Factors Worksheet

The Ideal Job Factors Worksheet lists up to 19 factors. Use the forced-ranking exercise to reduce and rank the total number of factors to no more than 10. Record those factors below, in order of importance.

To do this, compare each factor with all factors listed on the Ideal Job Factors Worksheet. Compare factor #1 with every other factor on your list. Which one is more important to you? Assign it a 1. Compare each factor with all the remaining factors.

Once you are done with this, take the second factor and compare it to the remaining factors on the list. Do the same comparisons with the third factor, and so on. When you are done, number the factors in descending order of importance, with the factor receiving the most votes of 1 at the top of the list. Record the top 10 factors below, with the top factor first.

Factor #1:

Factor #2:

Factor #3:

Factor #4:

Factor #5:

Factor #6:

Factor #7:

Factor #8:

Factor #9:

Factor #10:

Straw Men Worksheet

Review the following:

- The final set of priority factors or criteria from the self-assessment, as identified in the Ranking Ideal Job Factors Worksheet
- The career possibility you identified in the Possibilities chapter (Chapter 2)
- Any considerations from the Portfolio Career chapter (Chapter 5)

Pretend that you are an outside observer, reviewing this information about someone else. Identify up to five specific jobs that would be a great fit for this person. List them below. Complete a simple plus/minus evaluation of each job's fit with the priority job factors. Identify any missing information or gaps you need to address before you can complete the evaluation of this job.

Straw Man #1

- Job description

- Pluses
- Minuses
- Information gaps

Straw Man #2

- Job description

- Pluses
- Minuses
- Information gaps

Straw Men Worksheet (*Continued*)

Straw Man #3

- Job description

- Pluses
- Minuses
- Information gaps

Straw Man #4

- Job description

- Pluses
- Minuses
- Information gaps

Straw Man #5

- Job description

- Pluses
- Minuses
- Information gaps

Overall Evaluation and Selection of Alternatives

-
-
-
-

Competitive Advantages Worksheet

Use this worksheet to identify factual themes from your specific achievements and experiences. Accomplishments show what is distinctive about what you've achieved. Competitive advantages represent macro views of your brand: Use the following questions only as a starting point to help you define the themes.

Looking across your career, what is unique about your experience and skills? (Be factual.)

-
-
-

In what ways are your experience and skills broader than the competition's?

-
-
-

In what ways are your experience and skills deeper than the competition's?

-
-
-

Do you have unique industry or functional experience, or a combination?

-
-
-

Do you have unique or special and relevant skills and degrees?

-
-
-

Do you have experience with an industry leader?

-
-
-

Competitive Advantages Worksheet *(Continued)*

Do you have experience with different organizational stages?

-
-
-

Do you have experience with a special and relevant situation, project, or issue?

-
-
-

Do you have experience with the target market as a customer or a competitor?

-
-
-

Do you have experience with different kinds of companies?

-
-
-

Have you won any awards or received special recognition?

-
-
-

Do you have special training, talents, or memberships?

-
-
-

What other themes distinguish your background?

-
-
-

Why Hire You Worksheet

Important facts about the company:

-
-
-

My relevant career/job history:

-
-
-

My relevant accomplishments:

-
-
-

My competitive advantages:

-
-
-

Relevant anecdotes or examples to support competitive advantages:

-
-
-

Questions to ask:

-
-
-

Job Search Game Plan Worksheet

Ads

(List print and online ads and web sites you will check regularly.)

Search Firms and Employment Agencies

(List firms and contacts you will work with.)

Direct Targeting of Companies

(Identify target companies you will approach.)

Contacts

(List strategy and order of approach, if relevant, with different groups of your contacts, for example, contacts from a professional association, such as the New York City Bar Association; call about openings in their firm or contacts with other firms.)

Online Networking Tools

(Identify professional networks you will use, such as LinkedIn, Ryze.)

Self-Introduction

(Write a 30-second telephone introduction of who you are, who referred you, what you are looking for, why you are qualified for this target job, and what you want from the person you are contacting.)

Index

DATE DUE
